LISBON

CONTENTS

DISCOVER 6

EXPERIENCE 56

NEED TO KNOW 172

Left: The vast pavement map below the Monument to the Discoveries, Belém
Previous page: The Torre de Belém standing guard at the edge of the Tagus

DISCOVER

Sunrise over the Alfama's terracotta rooftops

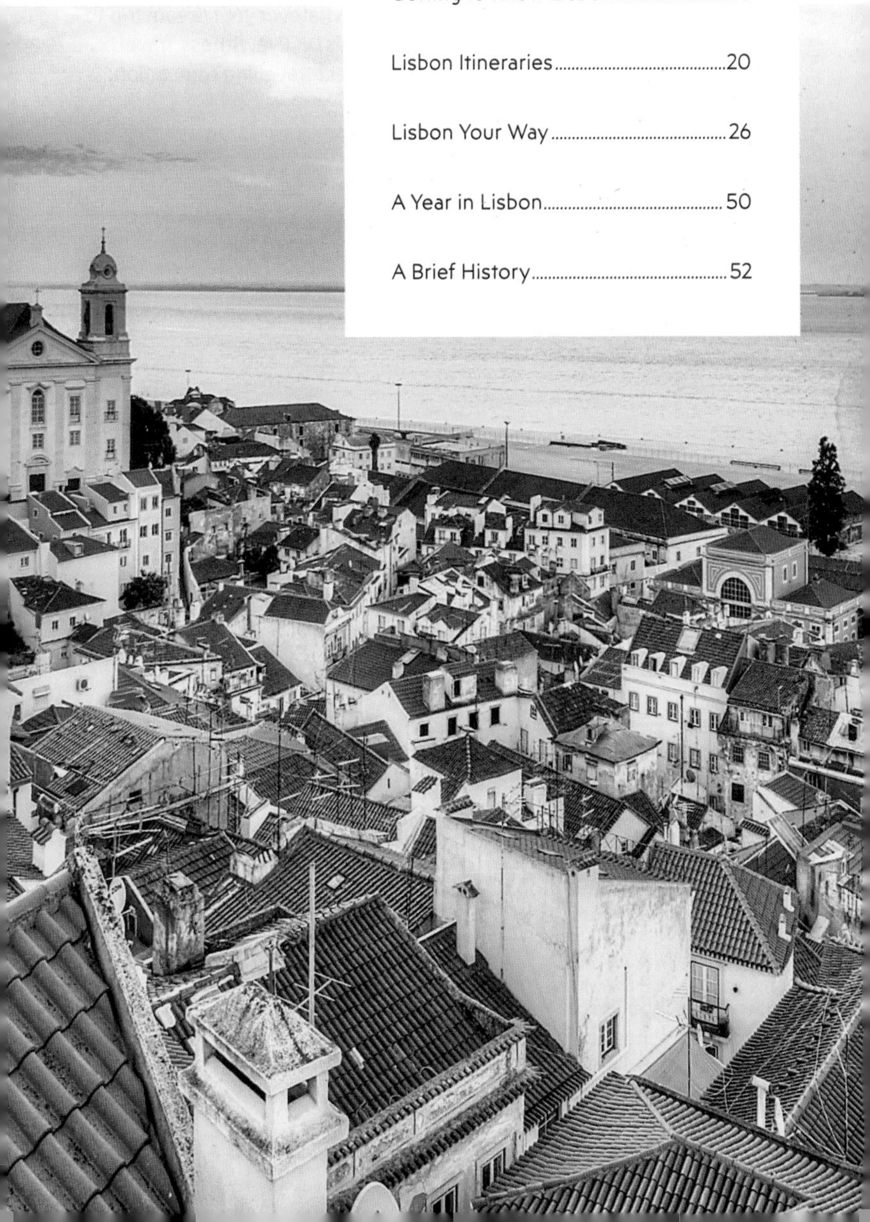

WELCOME TO
LISBON

Creamy custard tarts and the spine-tingling wail of traditional *fado* music. Steep, winding streets, with incredible views waiting at the top. World-class art, found within renowned museums or along *azulejo*-lined city streets. Whatever your dream trip to Lisbon includes, this DK Eyewitness Travel Guide will prove the perfect travelling companion.

1 The Elevador da Bica tram climbing a steep city street.

2 A golden curve of beach in Setúbal, on Lisbon's coast.

3 The vast Monument to the Discoveries in Belém.

4 A shaded *miradouro* overlooking Lisbon's rooftops.

Long lauded for its plentiful sunshine and excellent value, Lisbon's charms run far deeper. As befits one of the world's oldest cities, the capital of Portugal oozes history and tradition. Ancient buildings – from the Moorish to the Manueline – dot its diverse neighbourhoods (many of which can be traversed by jaunty wooden tram), while the brimming galleries of the Museu Nacional de Arte Antiga and the Museu Calouste Gulbenkian Founder's Collection also indicate a rich past. Beyond the city centre, day trips to palace-strewn Sintra or the golden shores of Lisbon's oft-forgotten beaches are within easy reach.

But the city also has a deserved reputation for European cool. Sample the vibrant nightlife of the Bairro Alto and Cais do Sodré districts, or peruse contemporary design collections at the eye-catching Museu de Arte, Arquitetura e Tecnologia (MAAT). While traditional refreshments – think fresh seafood and the country's ubiquitous fortified wine – are still very much a draw, a fast-developing foodie scene and rooftop bars that make the most of Lisbon's spectacular panoramas now offer travellers a slick alternative.

From the jumbled streets of the Alfama to atmospheric Belém and beyond, we've broken Lisbon down into easily navigable chapters, with detailed itineraries, expert local knowledge and colourful, comprehensive maps to help you plan the perfect visit. Whether you're staying for a weekend, a week, or longer, this Eyewitness guide will ensure that you see the very best the city has to offer. Enjoy the book, and enjoy Lisbon.

REASONS TO LOVE
LISBON

A stunning location, picturesque alleyways and streets to explore, friendly locals, excellent food, lively nightlife - and all in one of Europe's cheapest capital cities. What's not to love?

1 ALFAMA

There's no better way to get to know Lisbon than by exploring its oldest district (p58). Spend an afternoon wandering Alfama's winding alleyways, steep cobbled streets and hidden squares.

SEASIDE DAY TRIPS 2

There are some great beaches within easy reach of the city. South of the Tagus you can find miles of sandy shore - head here to bathe, surf or lunch on fresh fish by the sea.

3 CASTELO DE SÃO JORGE

Head to this sprawling hilltop citadel (p62) for fantastic views from its Moorish walls and the city's only camera obscura. The gardens are home to the castle's noisiest residents - peacocks!

MOSTEIRO DOS JERÓNIMOS 4

Spend a few hours admiring this vast monastery (p116), one of Lisbon's most elaborate and exuberant examples of Manueline architecture.

THE VIEWS 5

Lisbon's hilly setting results in stunning panoramas at almost every turn. Seek out the distinctive *miradouros*, tops of churches or grand open squares to find a photographer's paradise.

MOUTHWATERING PASTÉIS DE NATA 6

A trip to Lisbon feels incomplete without sampling one of the city's iconic custard tarts. Try them fresh from the oven and dusted with cinnamon.

SPECTACULAR SINTRA 7

An easy train ride outside the city, take a day to explore the extravagant palaces, lush gardens and dramatic wooded setting of this UNESCO World Heritage Site (p152).

VIBRANT NIGHTLIFE 8

At night, Lisbon's party districts leap into life, with bars and restaurants opening their doors and spilling into the streets. Head to the Bairro Alto (p92) or Cais do Sodré for all the action.

9 QUIRKY MUSEUMS

Lisbon has more than its share of unusual museums. Carriage fans should make for the Museu dos Coches (p119), while the Museu dos Azulejos is devoted to tiles and ceramics (p136).

10 FOOD FOR ALL

Lisbon caters for its visitors well, with options ranging from cheap and tasty traditional dishes to the city's burgeoning foodie scene *(p32)*. Arrive hungry, and dig in!

HISTORIC TRAM RIDES 11

The traditional tram 28 is a charming way to take in Lisbon's sights as it wends its way across the city, trundling up steep hills and down streets so narrow they almost scrape its sides.

COLOURFUL BUILDINGS 12

Lisbon is brimming with brightly coloured streets – whether façades patterned with traditional *azulejos*, pastel-painted houses or walls tattooed with street art.

EXPLORE
LISBON

This guide divides Lisbon into six colour-coded sightseeing areas: the four shown on this map, Beyond the Centre and the Lisbon Coast. Find out more about each area on the following pages.

Palácio Fronteira

Parque Florestal de Monsanto

Aqueduto das Águas Livres

CASELAS

CARAMÃO

BAIRRO DA AJUDA

Parque do Tapada do Ajuda

Cemitério dos Prazeres

ALTO DA AJUDA

Jardim Botânico da Ajuda

Palácio Nacional da Ajuda

RESTELO

Igreja da Memória

AJUDA

SANTO AMARO

Fundação Oriente Museu

ALCÂNTARA

Ermida de São Jerónimo

BELÉM

BELÉM
p112

Mosteiro dos Jerónimos

Palácio de Belém

Museu da Marinha

Museu Nacional dos Coches

Centro Cultural de Belém

MAAT – Museu de Arte, Arquitetura e Tecnologia

Padrão dos Descobrimentos

Ponte 25 Abril

Torre de Belém

Museu de Arte Popular

Tejo (Tagus)

| 0 metres | 750 |
| 0 yards | 750 |

N ↑

PORTO BRANDÃO

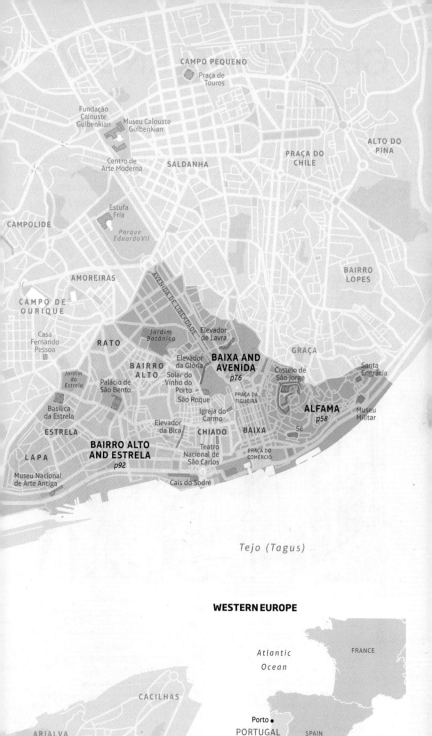

CAMPO PEQUENO

Praça de
Touros

Fundação
Calouste
Gulbenkian

Museu Calouste
Gulbenkian

Centro de
Arte Moderna

SALDANHA

PRAÇA DO
CHILE

ALTO DO
PINA

CAMPOLIDE

Estufa
Fría

Parque
Eduardo VII

AMOREIRAS

BAIRRO
LOPES

CAMPO DE
OURIQUE

Casa
Fernando
Pessoa

RATO

Jardim
Botânico

Elevador
de Lavra

GRAÇA

AVENIDA DE LIBERDADE

Jardim
da
Estrela

BAIRRO
ALTO

Palácio de
São Bento

Elevador
da Glória

Solar do
Vinho do
Porto

São Roque

BAIXA AND
AVENIDA
p76

Castelo de
São Jorge

Santa
Engrácia

Basílica
da Estrela

Igreja do
Carmo

PRAÇA DA
FIGUEIRA

ALFAMA
p58

Museu
Militar

ESTRELA

Elevador
da Bica

CHIADO

BAIXA

Sé

LAPA

BAIRRO ALTO
AND ESTRELA
p92

Teatro
Nacional de
São Carlos

PRAÇA DO
COMÉRCIO

Museu Nacional
de Arte Antiga

Cais do Sodré

Tejo (Tagus)

WESTERN EUROPE

CACILHAS

Atlantic
Ocean

FRANCE

ARIALVA

Porto

PORTUGAL

SPAIN

LISBON

ALMADA

Faro

Mediterranean
Sea

MOROCCO

ALGERIA

GETTING TO KNOW
LISBON

One of Europe's oldest and most attractive capitals, Lisbon has arrived into the 21st century with a vengeance; across the city, tradition jostles with cutting-edge architecture, a thumping nightlife and innovative restaurants. Some familiarity with each district will help when planning your trip.

PAGE 58

ALFAMA

Lisbon's oldest district, the labyrinthine Alfama tumbles downhill towards the river, hiding tiny bars, secret squares and a traditional way of life amid its narrow streets. This is the birthplace of *fado*, Portugal's mournful style of music, and the neighbourhood still hosts the Feira a Ladra, an authentic, twice-weekly street market packed with everything from postcards to antiques. Some of Lisbon's best viewpoints can also be found in the Alfama, with both the castle's ramparts and the Miradouro de Santa Luzia offering sweeping panoramas over the rest of the city.

Best for
Getting lost amid winding alleys and drinking in the city's atmosphere

Home to
The towering Castelo de São Jorge

Experience
Great views from the dome of Santa Engrácia, or an evening of music at a fado house

PAGE 76

BAIXA AND AVENIDA

The Baixa (lower town) is the heart of the city, comprising a grid of streets dotted with shops, cafés and boutiques, and culminating in the wide, waterfront Praça do Comércio. Running through the centre of the district is the pedestrianized Rua Augusta, where throngs of visitors and locals alike gather to shop, graze and gossip. Also in this area is the imposing Avenida da Liberdade, a wide avenue lined with Art Deco buildings that stretches all the way to Parque Eduardo VII.

Best for
Shopping and grand squares

Home to
The quirky Elevador de Santa Justa and the Praça do Comércio

Experience
Coffee and cakes at the Confeitaria Nacional, one of Lisbon's historic cafés

PAGE 92

BAIRRO ALTO AND ESTRELA

The Bairro Alto is Lisbon's nightlife district. By day it's relatively tranquil, but at night the neighbourhood comes alive with restaurants, cafés and bars that spill revellers out into the streets until the early hours. In Cais do Sodré you'll find the literally named Pink Street: once Lisbon's red light district, but now populated with stylish cocktail bars and clubs. The area offers culture, too, from Estrela's grand domed basilica to the impressive Museu Nacional de Arte Antiga in Lapa, home of Portugal's national art collection.

Best for
Lively restaurants and late-night bars

Home to
The Museu Nacional de Arte Antiga

Experience
Some of Lisbon's finest street food – from traditional to experimental – at the Time Out Market

→

BELÉM

PAGE 112

Once the embarkation point for Portugal's intrepid seafaring explorers, this scenic waterfront suburb is perhaps best known for its dramatic Manueline monuments from that period. Belém also features more modern attractions – such as the Berardo Collection of contemporary art and the imposing Padrão dos Descobrimentos – which combine with the neighbourhood's spacious streets and well-maintained, leafy parks to make it a pleasant place to wander.

Best for
Awe-inspiring architecture

Home to
The ornate Mosteiro dos Jerónimos and the Torre de Belém

Experience
A pastel de nata fresh out of the ovens at the original Belém bakery

BEYOND THE CENTRE

PAGE 130

Outside the city centre, there are still an impressive number of sights to be found. Parque Eduardo VII, with its sharply edged hedges and expansive *miradouro*, is a welcome green space for visitors to Lisbon, while the astounding collections of the nearby Museu Calouste Gulbenkian make for a rewarding visit. The brick-red Ponte 25 de Abril also stands in this area, stretching dramatically to the opposite bank of the Tagus, where the Christo Rei monument towers above the city.

Best for
Wide parks and a break from the city's bustle

Home to
The Museu Calouste Gulbenkian and the colourful Museu Nacional do Azulejo

Experience
Panoramic vistas from the viewing platform atop the Ponte 25 de Abril

THE LISBON COAST

With so much on offer in the city itself, it can be easy to forget that pristine beaches and shady woodland lie just a short distance away. Head northwest to the palace-dotted hills of Sintra, a must-do trip that can be squeezed into a day – although in this atmospheric town packed with spectacular architecture and exotic gardens, there's plenty to keep you there longer. Also within reach are the golden sands of Caparica and the Tróia Peninsula, while south of the Tagus sits the Serra da Arrábida, a wild, wooded mountain range that's ripe for exploring.

Best for
Fairy-tale palaces and surfing hotspots

Home to
Sintra, a UNESCO World Heritage Site, and the beautiful Palácio Nacional de Queluz

Experience
Gorgeously painted rooms in the Palácio Nacional de Sintra

←

1 Miradouro de Santa Luzia

2 Castelo de São Jorge

3 Tempting dishes at the Cantina Zé Avillez

4 Arco da Rua Augusta, leading to Praça do Comércio

Lisbon is a treasure trove of things to see and do, and its compact size means that much exploring can be done on foot. These itineraries will inspire you to make the most of your visit.

5 HOURS

If you only have a few hours in Lisbon, heading to the Castelo de São Jorge (p62) is an ideal way to take in an overview of the city. Spend one or two of your precious hours wandering the walls and ramparts of the hilltop citadel – and watch out for the peacocks, too. Next, meander downhill into the historic Alfama district (p58) – pausing en route at the Miradouro de Santa Luzia, a colourfully tiled viewpoint that offers splendid panoramas over the river. In Alfama, wander at will among the narrow cobbled streets, ducking beneath whatever archway takes your fancy. You're bound to emerge into a pretty square edged with flower-decked balconies, or beside a small church. Don't worry too much about getting lost; if you keep heading downhill, you'll emerge at the waterfront eventually. When you do, break for food at the Cantina Zé Avillez (p71), an informal resturant that serves up tasty, traditional Portuguese dishes with a contemporary twist, such as street-style octopus or veal trotters with chickpeas.

Once refreshed, it's a short walk from here to the vast, waterfront Praça do Comércio (p80). Descend the marble steps on the square's southern side to marvel at the breadth and beauty of the Tagus, or – if you're eager to experience more of Lisbon's unmatched viewpoints – head to the north side and get a lift to the top of the Arco da Rua Augusta. After taking in the bustle of the streets below, immerse yourself in them; spend the rest of your time wandering the grid of streets in the Baixa (p76), many of which are named after the historic shops that once lined them. The most famous of these is Rua Augusta (p88), an attractive, pedestrianized avenue that teems with shops, cafés and street performers. End your stroll with an apéritif and a pastry – the iconic pastéis de nata (custard tarts) will undoubtedly be on offer – in one of the streetside cafés, and simply enjoy watching local Lisbon life as it passes by.

←

1 Torre de Belém

2 Museu Calouste Gulbenkian

3 Perfectly baked *patéis de nata*

4 PARK bar, Bairro Alto

2 DAYS

Day 1

Morning Start your day with breakfast at one of the cafés on Praça da Figueira (p88) or neighbouring Rossio (p84) – Confeitaria Nacional (www.confeitaria nacional.com) has a great pastry selection. Once fully fuelled, wander through the Baixa's pedestrianized streets to the quirky, Gothic-style Elevador de Santa Justa (p82). Take the lift up to the hilltop Museu do Carmo (p100), an archaeological museum housed in a Carmelite church, whose graceful ruined arches stand out against the city skyline. Spend an hour or two browsing the boutique collection, before heading through the elegant Chiado district towards the waterfront.

Afternoon Here, the Time Out Market (p107) in Cais do Sodré is a great place for a pick-and-mix lunch. The selection on offer is huge – just pick your stall, choose a dish and snag a seat at one of the huge communal tables. After lunch, hop on the metro to the Museu Calouste Gulbenkian (p132), where exploring the sprawling collection of artworks will quickly eat up the rest of your afternoon.

Evening Head back towards the city centre and spend the evening in the lively bars and restaurants of Bairro Alto. Grab a table at PARK (Calçada do Combro 58, above the car park) to make the most of Lisbon's stunning skyline. This rooftop bar overlooks the river, with tasty burgers on the menu and a strong line in cocktails.

Day 2

Morning Aim for a bright and early start in order to make the most of Belém, one of Lisbon's prettiest suburbs. Take a short tram ride or the train along the waterfront, and head first to the Mosteiro dos Jerónimos (p116). This elaborately decorated monastery demands at least an hour or two to explore properly – the refectory's azulejo panels and the cloister are particularly spectacular. Next, cross through the gardens to the towering 52-m- (170-ft-) high Padrão dos Descobrimentos (p122), and take the high-speed lift to the top for great views over the monastery and the river.

Afternoon Nearby, the colourful Rua Viera Portuense is home to a number of excellent restaurants where you can lunch at outdoor tables. Skip pudding here and cross the road to the Antiga Confeitaria de Belém bakery (p123) – for where better to sample Portugal's iconic tarts than the café in which they were first created? Walk off your sweet treat along the waterfront to reach the Torre de Belém (p118), worth a visit to admire its intricate stonework.

Evening Next, take a look round the impressive Museu Colecção Berardo (p123), where the modern art on display includes pieces by the likes of Dalí, Picasso and Andy Warhol. End your evening in Enoteca de Belém, a tiny wine bar tucked down Travessa Marta Pinto with delicious seafood options and a vast wine list.

←

1 Oceanário de Lisboa's impressive main aquarium

2 Parque Eduardo VII

3 Playing in the surf at the Costa da Capirica

4 Sintra's Palácio Nacional

5 DAYS

Day 1

Morning Start your day at the church of Santa Engrácia, whose marbled interior houses tombs of the Portuguese great and the good (p65). If it's Tuesday or Saturday, wander over to the nearby Feira da Ladra market (p64).

Afternoon After lunch, catch the iconic tram 28 for a scenic route to the Museu Nacional de Arte Contemporânea do Chiado (p102). You'll need at least a couple of hours to explore the impressive exhibition, which is Portugal's largest collection of contemporary art.

Evening Jump back onto the tram 28 to the Basílica da Estrela (p106). The basilica's roof terrace gives great views over the city, while a stroll in the neighbouring Estrela gardens is a relaxing way to end the evening.

Day 2

Morning Take an early train to Sintra (p152), where your first stop is the Palácio Nacional (p154), a former royal residence.

Afternoon Next, take the bus up the hill to the flamboyant Palácio da Pena (p156). Have your camera at the ready for great views across the coast and back towards Lisbon from the walls and ramparts.

Evening Finish your day at the Palácio de Monserrate (p162). As the light begins to fade, stroll through the beautiful landscaped Monserrate Gardens.

Day 3

Morning Venture northeast to Parque das Nações (p144), where a ride on the cable car affords great views over the river. Then head to the Oceanário de Lisboa, one of Europe's largest aquariums, which is home to some 8,000 fish and marine animals (p144).

Afternoon Catch a bus along the riverfront to the Museu Nacional do Azulejo (p136), where you'll find a breath-taking collection of Portugal's most unique art form.

Evening When you're all tiled out, head back into the city centre, to Rossio's Bonjardim restaurant for another Portuguese speciality of spit-roast chicken with piri-piri sauce (p88).

Day 4

Morning Take the bus from Praça do Areeiro to the Costa da Caparica, where you'll find miles of long, sandy beach perfect for bathing, surfing or just chilling (p163).

Afternoon Enjoy a seafood or barbecued fish lunch at one of the restaurants or cafés overlooking the beach.

Evening On the way back, ride the bus to Cacilhas, and catch a ferry back to Cais do Sodré, enjoying the expansive views of Cristo Rei (p138), the Ponte 25 do Abril and the Lisbon waterfront.

Day 5

Morning Walk up through the formal Parque Eduardo VII (p139) to El Corte Inglés, Lisbon's largest department store, for some serious shopping (p141).

Afternoon Stop for afternoon tea in the nearby Art Deco Pastelaria Versailles (p145), then wander back into the centre of town along the grand Avenida da Liberdade (p84).

Evening In the evening, head for the Alfama district, and settle into dinner accompanied by some soulful fado in one of the neighbourhood's famous fado restaurants (p43).

Contemporary Collections

Modern art fans are well catered for in Lisbon. The Calouste Gulbenkian's Modern Collection *(p135)* brings leading Portuguese contemporary artists together with international names such as David Hockney and Antony Gormley. The impressive Berardo Collection, meanwhile, features the likes of Andy Warhol and Mark Rothko *(p123)*, while the fantastic Casa das Historias in Cascais *(p163)* is dedicated to the haunting works of Paula Rego.

$\rightarrow$

Bright, wide galleries in the Calouste Gulbenkian's Modern Collection

Did You Know?

The Museu Calouste Gulkenbian houses the world's largest collection of René Lalique jewellery.

LISBON FOR
ART LOVERS

Lisbon is fast becoming one of Europe's most creative cities, home to works of art that range from ancient sculptures through contemporary design-based collections to colourful splashes of street art. Today artists flock here for the affordable housing and studio rents, resulting in a vibrant, innovative art scene.

Museu Calouste Gulbenkian – Founder's Collection

One of Lisbon's most extensive museums, this is a must for any art connoisseur. It originated as the impeccable private collection of Calouste Gulbenkian *(p132)*, which he bequeathed to his adopted country on his death in 1955. Explore galleries filled with pieces from Ancient Egypt through to the 20th century, including Chinese porcelain and priceless paintings from big hitters such as Rembrandt and Monet.

$\leftarrow$

Pieces of sculpture on display in the Museu Calouste Gulbenkian Founder's Collection

Street Art

Azulejos aside, Lisboetas have a reputation for another way of brightening up their streets: graffiti art. Skilled displays can be seen across the city, from the council-approved, open-air "gallery" in Calçada da Glória to the heavily painted walls of LX Factory *(p141)*. Large-scale works by artist Alexandre Farto, better known as Vhils, can often be found on the sides of industrial buildings.

→

Colourful street art adorning walls on a Lisbon street

Colonial Art

Portugal's past as a ruling nation has resulted in a collection of bounty from across the globe. The Museu Nacional de Arte Antiga *(p96)* acts as the country's national gallery, showcasing a vast array of works from both mainland Portugal and its former colonies and trading partners. Don't miss Nuno Gonçalves' *St Vincent* polyptych.

←

A visitor admiring porcelain at the Museu Nacional de Arte Antiga

Above the Crowds

For great views over the Praça do Comércio, one of Lisbon's sprawling plazas that sits right on the water's edge, take a lift followed by a narrow spiral staircase to the top of the Arco da Rua Augusta. From here you'll also have a bird's-eye view of downtown Baixa – with its terracotta rooftops and grid-like streets – and all the action along the lively Rua Augusta, where street performers gather to entertain the daily crowds.

←
Ornate details atop the Arco da Rua Augusta

LISBON FOR
PHOTOGRAPHERS

Set on seven hills covered in a patchwork of multicoloured houses and offering views across the wide Tagus river, Lisbon is easily one of Europe's most photogenic cities. With bright sunshine and blue skies only adding to its beauty, here are some of our favourite spots.

LISBON'S MIRADOUROS

All across Lisbon you'll find dramatic *miradouros,* or viewpoints, where the Portuguese gather to admire their city from a particularly excellent vantage point. Some (such as Santa Luzia) feature traditional tiles and pergolas, while others are tucked-away shady spots (Miradouro da Graça) or larger, park-like spaces (São Pedro de Alcântara). Whatever their differences in location or style, all *miradouros* make for excellent photo opportunities, so seek them out with your camera at the ready.

King of the Castle

Looming spectacularly above the city is Alfama's Castelo de São Jorge, from where visitors can take in a jumble of terracotta tiled roofs laid out below. The classic view is looking west from the castle's battlements – it takes in everything from the grand squares of the Baixa to the river, and the Barrio Alto on the opposite hill.

→
View back over the city from the castle's walls

Ponte 25 de Abril

Search for #lisbon on Instagram, and this Golden Gate lookalike is sure to pop up. For an unusual angle, head to the roof terrace of the Rio Maravilha bar *(p41)* in the LX Factory. Here a colourful statue mimics the Cristo Rei on the river's opposite bank, with the bridge stretching between the two.

→

The mighty Ponte 25 de Abril, lit up at night and stretching across the Tagus

Tram Spotting

No budding photographer should leave Lisbon without a shot of the iconic tram 28, which has become one of the best-known symbols of the city. A great place to catch the bright yellow tram as it trundles through the Alfama's cobbled alleys is along Rua das Escolas Gerais, where the road is so narrow passengers can almost touch the buildings lining the street.

←

The popular tram 28

Tile-tastic

Lisbon's traditional ceramic tiles are ubiquitous in the city; you're likely to find buildings clad in colourful *azulejos* on almost every corner. Head to the house on Baixa's Largo Rafael Bordalo Pinheiro to snap its gold-and-orange façade, or for classic blue-and-white tiles try 68 Calçada Marquês Abrantes in Bairro Alto. *Azulejos* experienced a resurgence of popularity in the 1950s, and many metro stations dating from this time also feature colourful designs.

→

Azulejos adorn a house in Baixa's Largo Rafael Bordalo Pinheiro

💬 INSIDER TIP
Lunch Time

Even the fussiest of fussy eaters will enjoy Lisbon's ubiquitous spit-roast chicken and chips. Head to Bonjardim (*p88*), known locally as "Rei dos Frangos" (King of Chickens), to sample this simple but delicious Portuguese speciality.

LISBON FOR
FAMILIES

Beneath Lisbon's stylish reputation is a city bubbling with energy and captivating quirks. Children are welcomed wherever they go, and the outdoor style of living and host of interactive museums make this an ideal destination for families.

Getting Around

Even travelling around Lisbon can be exciting, with a wide range of unusual transport options on offer. The intriguing *elevadores* (street lifts) have been gliding up the city's steepest hills since the 19th century, as has the Santa Justa lift (*p82*), which is topped by a breathtaking viewing platform. Weave through the tight streets of the Alfama on the iconic tram 28, or catch the public ferry to Cacilhas to admire Lisbon's skyline from across the water. If your kids have a head for heights, take to the skies on a cable car at the Parque das Nações (*p144*), from where you can see one of Europe's longest bridges stretched out ahead of you.

Lisbon's cable car running along the river's edge ↑

Interactive Exhibits

Lisbon's many museums offer hands-on exhibits that adults and children alike will love – try the Museu da Carris, where kids can learn about the city's public transport system while clambering over vintage buses (p141). There's also the Oceanário (p144), one of Europe's largest aquariums, or the Museu da Água (p144), a captivating attraction that is located in an eerie underground reservoir – and offers even spookier tunnel tours.

← Oceanário's fish-filled tanks delighting visitors

TOP 5 FREE KIDS' ACTIVITIES

Street Theatre
Watch the performers on Rua Augusta (p88).

Parque das Nações
Cool off in the gardens' fountains (p144).

Feed the Ducks
Befriend the birds in Jardim da Estrela (p106).

Gulbenkian Gardens
Run around these quirky museum gardens (p132).

On Top of the World
Visit the huge map at Belém's Padrão dos Descobrimentos (p122).

↑ Bodyboarding on the perfect wave at Caparica's beach

Outdoor Fun

In a sunshine-saturated city like Lisbon, there are plenty of outdoor activities to keep little ones entertained. Take a train along the coast to the golden sands of Estoril for safe sea swimming, or head to Caparica's huge beach, ideal for bodyboarding or surfing. Back in town, hire bikes near Belém and let the family loose along the traffic-free riverfront.

Cycling up ↑
Lisbon's steep
cobbled streets

To Market, To Market

As supermarkets increase their hold, Lisbon's old-style food markets have declined - but there are still a few to be found. Try Alcântara's Mercado Rosa Argulhas or Saldanha's Mercado 31 de Janeiro, where traditional stallholders sell local meat, fish, fruit and vegetables. The city's most famous historic market, the Mercado da Ribeira, was relaunched in 2014 as the hugely popular Time Out Market (p107). Alongside a few original stalls, the market also houses an array of contemporary kiosks, serving everything from cheap and cheerful street food to dishes by some of the city's top chefs.

→

Food kiosks lining the edges of Time Out Market's cavernous hall

LISBON FOR
FOODIES

Portugal's capital brings together great ingredients from all over the country, offering an abundance of fresh fish and lush vegetables. Previously under-rated as a foodie destination, a new cohort of creative young chefs has revitalized Lisbon's culinary scene. Here's what to seek out during your visit.

LISBON FOR VEGETARIANS

Only a few years ago, vegetarians in Lisbon would have been limited to omelette, chips and salad, but today an excellent array of meat-free restaurants can be found. Try Os Tibetanos (tibetanos.com) - the city's oldest veggie restaurant, which serves Tibetan dishes - Terra (restaurante terra.pt) or Jardim dos Sentidos (jardimdos entidos.com) for tasty vegan options. Be wary, however, if waiters suggest a bowl of caldo verde; it's a delicious vegetable soup, but often has slices of chorizo floating in it.

Coffee and Cakes

The Portuguese are well known for their sweet tooth, and Lisbon is home to some excellent old-style cafés filled with rows of tempting treats. It's the custard-filled, flaky pastel de nata, however, that has firmly established itself as the city's iconic pastry. Head to the Antiga Confeitaria de Belém bakery (p123) to sample the original recipe, warm from the oven.

→

A line of customers gathers at Belém's famous bakery

EAT

For modern cuisine,
try these eateries.

Mini-Bar
◉M7 ⬛Rua António
Maria Cardoso 58
🌐minibar.pt

€€€

**Santa Clara
dos Cogumelos**
◉Y2 ⬛Mercado de
Santa Clara 🌐santa
claradoscoguelos.com

€€€

Prado
◉W3 ⬛Travessa das
Pedras Negras 🌐prado
restaurante.com

€€€

← A perfectly
baked batch
of Lisbon's
famous
custard tarts

↑ A tempting
bowl of
bacalhau, a
Portuguese
speciality

Portuguese Tradition

Lisbon still has plenty of restaurants and
cervejarias (beer halls) that serve up
hearty portions of traditional food. Akin to
a national dish is *bacalhau* - dried, salted
cod that can be prepared in seemingly
endless varieties. Other native favourites
include *frango à piri-piri* - fiery barbecued
chicken - and *arroz de marisco*, seafood
cooked in a tasty rice stew.

Museum Gardens

Some of the city's loveliest green spaces are its museum gardens, many of which can be enjoyed without having to pay the museum entry fee. Sandwiched between the Founder's Collection and the modern art museum is the Gulbenkian Garden *(p132)*, a haven of tranquil, statue-dotted lawns. The gardens of the Museu Nacional de Arte Antiga *(p96)* are similarly picturesque, with neat lawns that stretch down to overlook the river.

→

Locals relaxing in the Museu Calouste Gulbenkian's landscaped gardens

LISBON FOR
GREEN SPACES

Though perhaps better known for its hot sunshine and colourful buildings, Lisbon offers plenty of cool green patches amid its bustling streets. Locals gather in these parks and gardens to chat, picnic and escape the hectic pace of city life.

Parque Eduardo VII

Lisbon's largest park, and perhaps its most iconic green space, this long stretch of garden runs through the centre of the city *(p139)*. Ornamental box hedges top the pristine lawns, while shaded, wilder areas are tucked away at either side. Once you've had your fill of the lower slope, tackle the steep walk up to the top of the park to find an open *miradouro* that gives fantastic views over the city.

Sun setting over the geometric hedges of Parque Eduardo VII ↑

Shady Sintra

Historically popular with the Portuguese royal family as an escape from the summer heat of Lisbon, Sintra's wooded ravines and cool greenery do not disappoint today. Spend some time exploring the quiet walks that wind through the town's surrounding hills, or head for the more cultivated beauty of Monserrate's exotic palace gardens (p162). The latter is one of the richest examples of a botanic garden in Portugal and home to plant species from all over the world. Plants are organized according to the geographical areas from which they originated, so you're always likely to find something in bloom.

← A pictureseque park knoll in the wooded hills of Sintra

TOP 4 SECRET ESCAPES

Jardim da Cerca da Graça
A charming space just north of Alfama, beside the old Graça convent.

Jardim do Príncipe Real
This romantic, shady square lies just off Bairro Alto's main street (p103).

Jardim da Estrela
A mid-19th-century garden with an attractive central pavilion and a craft fair at weekends (p106).

Parque do Tejo
Sprawling along the south bank of the Tagus, in the shadow of the Ponte 25 de Abril, these gardens are home to diverse flora and fauna.

Botanical Gardens

Lisbon is well known for the lush botanic gardens that dot its districts, offering serene green oases away from the bustle and heat of the city. Tucked off busy Rua da Escola Politécnica is the sprawling - if somewhat unkempt - Jardim Botânico (p83), home to some 20,000 plant species. Further out, Belém offers two stunning gardens. The Jardim Botânico Tropical (p120) is ideally located next to the Mosteiro dos Jerónimos, and holds rare and endangered tropical flora. Nearby is the more formal Jardim Botânico da Ajuda (p127), which is Lisbon's oldest botanical garden, dating from 1768.

→ Visitors strolling in the attractive Jardim da Estrela

Cost-Free Culture

Seek out free museums and sights across the city – perhaps explore the austere grandeur of the Sé cathedral (you'll have to pay to visit the cloister and treasury) or phone ahead to book an underground tour at the Núcleo Arqueológico *(p89)*. Other sites offer free entry at certain times, such as the Museu Calouste Gulbenkian *(p132)*, which is free after 2pm on Sundays.

←

Contemporary sculptures in the Museu Calouste Gulbenkian's Modern Collection

LISBON ON A
SHOESTRING

One of Europe's least expensive capitals, Lisbon is an excellent destination for travellers on a budget. None of the city's attractions will break the bank – and food, drink and transport are all reasonably priced – but with a little planning your money can go even further.

Two Feet, Two Wheels

The city's central area is compact enough to see on foot – just make sure to pack comfortable footwear for tackling the many hills! If you're keen to pick up more speed, inexpensive bike hire companies in Belém and Cascais are ideal for exploring these relatively flat districts.

↑ Visitors strolling Lisbon's bustling streets on foot

Take a Ferry Trip

Situated as the city is on the banks of the Tagus, it's no wonder that boat rides prove perenially popular with visitors to Lisbon. Avoid tourist-trap river cruises and instead take the cheaper commuter ferry from Cais do Sodré to Cacilhas – it offers the same spectacular views for a fraction of the price, and the experience feels delightfully authentic. On the other side of the river await a wealth of excellent seafood restaurants.

←

A passenger
ferry crossing
the Tagus

> ◯ INSIDER TIP
> **Drink Local**
>
> Stick to local brand beers, wines and spirits, which tend to be the cheapest but are invariably good. Ordering drinks from the counter or bar at a café, rather than being served at a table, will also help to save money.

→

Locals enjoying
Portuguese specialities
(inset), in lively Alfama

Large Lunches

Making lunch your main meal is a good way to cut back on food costs; many of the city's restaurants do an excellent value *menu do dia* (menu of the day) at lunch time, which usually includes bread, soup, a main course, pudding and a drink. If you wander a little further off the beaten track to where the locals are eating, you're likely to pay as little as €10 a head.

Underground Art Deco

Some of the city's most fantastic contemporary and Art Deco tiles can be found on the walls of Lisbon's metro stations. Modernist artist Maria Keil decorated 19 stations, and is credited with reviving widespread enthusiasm for *azulejos*; head to Alvalade to take in some of her wonderfully colourful panels. Metro do Oriente displays maritime-themed tiles by artists from around the world, and Campo Grande is home to some intriguing 18th-century *azulejo* figures by Eduardo Nery.

→

A Chegança by Luiz Ventura (1994) in Restauradores station

LISBON'S
AZULEJOS

Decorative tiles were first brought to Portugal by the Moors in the 8th century, but became an art form as the uniquely Portuguese *azulejos* under Manuel I in the 16th century. Ceramic designs brighten buildings throughout Lisbon, adorning everything from historic palaces to modern-day metro stations.

Tiles and Styles

Lisbon's *azulejos* vary radically according to the period in which they were painted. Head to Sintra to see some of Portugal's earliest Moorish-style tiles, where the Palácio Nacional's Sala dos Árabes (p154) is decorated with fine green geometric examples. Back in central Lisbon, the Palácio Fronteira (p146) is lined with beautiful 17th-century Delft ceramics, while the church of São Vicente da Fora (p64) displays tile panels illustrating the fables of La Fontaine.

←

Spectacular blue *azulejos* adorning the chapel and terrace of the Palácio Fronteira

Factory Visit

Those keen to see *azulejo*-making in action should head to Fábrica Sant'Anna, a ceramics factory in the streets behind the Praça do Comércio *(p80)*. Founded in 1741, the factory still produces handmade tiles and other pottery using traditional techniques. Visitors can watch artists paint the tiles by hand, before snapping up a bargain in the attached shop.

→

An artist carefully hand-painting a tile design

Museu Nacional do Azulejo

Unmissable for any *azulejo* addict, this museum – housed in the former Madre de Deus convent – provides an overview of the art form's history and showcases some stunning examples *(p136)*. Moorish tiles through to 20th-century pieces are all on display.

→

Colourful ceramics in the Museu Nacional do Azulejo

Lisbon Live

While most visitors are keen to experience Lisbon's famed *fado (p42)*, the city also offers plenty of opportunities to hear other types of live music. For jazz, head to the Hot Clube de Portugal – one of Europe's oldest jazz clubs – or seek out jazz festivals throughout the year, such as the Cool Jazz Fest in July. Altice Arena in the Parque das Nações is the place for big-name international bands, while Coliseu dos Recreios and Campo Pequeno bullring host top Portuguese artists.

→

Sharon Jones and the Dap-Kings performing at the Cool Jazz Fest in Cascais

LISBON
AFTER DARK

Portugal's capital offers visitors a thriving nightlife. As the sun sets, locals pack into street cafés and restaurants for an evening of food, drink and conviviality, before the late-night bars and thumping clubs take over till dawn.

A Night in Bairro Alto

With its myriad bars and restaurants spilling into the quarter's narrow cobbled streets, the Bairro Alto is Lisbon's best-known area for nightlife. Spend an evening sampling its traditional drinking holes, which boast low prices and late opening hours. In recent years, more alternative crowds have migrated to nearby regenerated areas such as Cais do Sodré, with its lively Pink Street *(p17)*, and Santos, which offers numerous bars and clubs.

←

Locals enjoying dinner outside in Bairro Alto's Calçada do Duque street

TOP
4

LISBON NIGHTCLUBS

Lux
Lisbon's long-standing premier nightspot (www.luxfragil.com).

Ministerium Club
House and electro in a sleek interior (www.ministeriumclub.com).

Music Box
Live alternative and ' world music bar (www.musicboxlisboa.com).

B.Leza Clube
Upbeat live African and Brazilian music club (+ 210 106 837).

Rooftop Cocktails
Sky-high bars have sprung up across the city, creating plenty of places to sip an ice-cold caipirinha while taking in the scenery. Both trendy PARK, a roof-top bar with DJs and comfy sofas *(p23)*, and riverside cocktail bar, Rio Maravilha (www.riomaravilha.pt), offer stunning panoramas of the city.

←

Expansive views of Lisbon at PARK bar's rooftop terrace

Show Time!
Theatre is popular in Lisbon, with many of the city's playhouses located along the Rua das Portas de Santo Antão. Lisbon's most historic theatre is the 18th-century Teatro Nacional Dona Maria II, which puts on plays such as *Waiting for Godot* – though usually in Portuguese. International audiences may prefer the opera at the Teatro Nacional de São Carlos, or ballet at the Companhia Nacional de Bailado.

→

Teatro Nacional Dona Maria II

Musicians performing at ↑
Clube de Fado in the
Alfama district

LISBON FOR
FADO FANS

Literally translated as "fate", *fado* is a genre of music peculiar to Portugal that expresses longing and sorrow. The people of Lisbon have nurtured this poignant music in back-street cafés and restaurants for over 150 years, and it has altered little in that time.

Museu do Fado

Set in a former bathhouse, this should be the first port of call for anyone looking to learn about the cultural and historical significance of *fado* (p66). Exhibits trace the rise of *fado*, which originated in the 1800s in some of Portugal's poorest streets and swelled to the iconic art form that is celebrated internationally today. Alongside photographs and paintings, there are recordings of famous singers on display, and a great selection of CDS in the shop.

→

Visitors being treated to
a live performance at the
Museu do Fado

Fado Houses

The haunting melodies of *fado* can still be heard in designated "houses" throughout Lisbon, most of which offer a meal and drinks during the show (although it is considered impolite to make noise while the singer and guitarist are performing). Lisbon's best *fado* houses tend to be run by *fadistas* themselves. Based on a love of music and on relationships with other performers, such houses offer an authentic taste of the traditional art form. Alfama, the birthplace of the genre, is host to myriad *fado* venues, but Bairro Alto's maze of bars also holds gems such as Travessa da Queimada's Café Luso, which first opened in 1927 and hosted the legendary *fadista*, Amalia Rodrigues.

← *Azulejos* depicting José Malhôa's *fadista* and listener

EAT

Dine at these top *fado* restaurants.

Clube de Fado
🅟X4 🅐R. de São João da Praça 86 🅦clube-de-fado.com

€€€

Parreirinha de Alfama
🅟X3 🅐Beco do Espírito Santo 1 🅦parrei rinhadealfama.com

€€€

Tasca do Chico
🅟M6 🅐R. do Diário de Notícias 39

€€€

→ Street performers playing *fado vadio*

Fado Vadio

Translating as bohemian or vagabond *fado*, this strand of the art form is performed outside of the dedicated, professional *fado* houses. Largely sung by amateurs, performances tend to be less slick than in the *fado* houses, but more emotionally charged. Head for the jumbled *tascas* and bars of Alfama to hear true *fado vadio*.

THE GUITARRA

Specific to Portuguese culture, the *guitarra* is a flat-backed instrument shaped like a mandolin, with twelve strings. It has evolved from a simple 19th-century design into a finely decorated piece, sometimes inlaid with mother-of-pearl. An essential ingredient of good *fado*, the *guitarra* echoes and enhances the singer's melody line.

Table Wines

Portuguese table wines have traditionally been viewed as cheap and cheerful, but the influence of international viniculturists and new wine-making techniques have resulted in the production of top-class wines. The light, slightly sparkling *Vinho Verde* – or "green wine" – from the north is the best known, but there are plenty of full-bodied wines produced in the Lisbon area. Estremadura to the north, Ribatejo to the east, and Palmela and Setúbal to the south guarantee a strong selection.

→

Inspecting fine wine in a cellar in Lisbon's Alfama district

1756

The Douro Valley was demarcated by the Marquês de Pombal in this year.

LISBON
RAISE A GLASS

Although still overshadowed by the excellence and fame of port, Portugal's alcoholic alternatives deserve to be taken seriously. From Madeira wine and sparkling *Vinho Verde* to a growing craft beer scene, you'll find plenty to please the palate in Lisbon.

Fortified Wines

Portugal's best-known fortified wine is undoubtedly port, a tipple so popular it has come to be synonymous with the country. Grown in the Douro Valley, both red and white grape varieties are used to make different versions of the drink. White port tends to be drier than ruby or tawny ports, more like a sherry, and is often drunk cold as an apéritif. Madeira, of course, produces its own eponymous fortified wine, which is aged in wooden barrels and ranges from dry to sweet dessert wines.

←

Sampling varieties of port from Portugal's Douro Valley

TOP 5 ALTERNATIVE SPIRITS TO TRY

Macieira
Portugal's most popular domestic brandy.

Medronho
A potent and fruity firewater from the wild strawberry tree.

Bagaço
A spirit made from grape skins that can be drunk neat, or added to coffee to give it more of a kick.

Brandymel
A liqueur that includes honey and mountain herbs.

Licor Beirão
A liqueur flavoured with aromatic seeds and herbs.

← Pouring a shot of *ginjinha* cherry liqueur

Ginjinha
Lisbon's most unusual drink is a liqueur called *ginjinha*, made from sour cherries, *aguardente* brandy and sugar. It's typically taken just before or after meals, and one of the best places to sample this Portuguese speciality is a tiny street bar just off Rossio, named A Ginjinha. You're expected to glug back the sweet liqueur in one, then finish off the tongue-twistingly sour cherry at the bottom.

Portuguese Beers
Bars in Lisbon tend to serve one of two Portuguese lager-like beers: Sagres and Super Bock. For craft beer, you'll have to look a little harder – but it does exist and is rapidly growing in popularity. Porto-based Sovina, the country's first craft beer company, produces a variety of regular beers (including IPA and stout) plus seasonal specials, while offerings at quirkily named Mean Sardine include a popular American pale ale.

→ Friends enjoying an alfresco drink at a café in Rossio square

Did You Know?

Visitors can walk across the curving roof of MAAT to enjoy stunning views of the Tagus.

LISBON'S
ARCHITECTURE

Shaped by its rich history, Portugal's capital hosts a variety of adventurous architecture. Design enthusiasts will find plenty to feast their eyes on – from the Arabic influence of the Moors through the distinctive Manueline style, to dramatic New State buildings and striking contemporary structures.

ÁLVARO SIZA VIEIRA

Álvaro Siza Vieira (born 1933) is Portugal's most famous architect. He won the prestigious Pritzker Prize in 1992 for his renovation of Lisbon's Chiado district, after it was largely destroyed by a fire in 1988. Known for his Modernist clean lines and simplicity, he also worked on the Portuguese National Pavilion - famed for its enormous sagging concrete canopy - built for Expo 98.

Twentieth-Century and New State Structures

In the 1930s, Portugal's dictator António Salazar promoted a public works programme; many of the buildings erected in line with this were Modernist concrete structures with nationalistic touches, designed to double as symbols of propaganda. Examples today include the Monument to the Discoveries in Belém (p122), an austere monument embellished with sculptures of heroes from history, and the towering Cristo Rei (p138), a vast statue of Christ facing the Tagus.

← The imposing Monument to the Discoveries

Contemporary Architecture

Modern Lisbon boasts buildings by some of the world's leading contemporary architects. In the Parque das Nações (p144), you'll find Peter Chermayeff's striking modernist oceanarium and Santiago Calatrava's cavernous Oriente station. Cascais offers the terracotta towers of the Casa das Histórias, designed by Eduardo Souto de Moura (p163). Lisbon's latest stand-out structure is the sleek MAAT (p126), a museum showcasing the best in architecture and design.

←

The curvaceous MAAT, designed by Amanda Levete Architects

TOP 5 GEMS OF ARCHITECTURE

Santa Engrácia
This soaring dome is the national pantheon (p65).

Aqueduto das Águas Livres
A 58-km aqueduct dating from 1748 (p146).

Igreja do Carmo
The Gothic ruins of a Carmelite church (p100).

Basílica da Estrela
A Baroque and Neo-Classical convent (p106).

Casa do Alentejo
A palace known for its Neo-Moorish decor (p91).

Manueline Designs

This style emerged during the reign of Manuel I (1495–1521), and is also known as Portuguese late Gothic. It heavily features maritime motifs, inspired by Portugal's Age of Discovery. Key examples are the exquisitely pattened Mosteiro dos Jerónimos (p116), and the iconic Torre de Belém (p118).

→

Ornate cloisters of the Mosteiro dos Jerónimos

Moorish Lisbon

Ruled by the Moors from the 8th to the 12th century, Lisbon still bears traces of their distinctive architectural style. Defensive walls endure, and even the winding, step-strewn streets are a Moorish legacy, the layout devised to disrupt assaults from the river. Nearby Sintra (p152) is home to the spectacular Castelos dos Mouros and the Moorish-inspired Palácio de Monserrate.

→

Tenth-century Castelos dos Mouros, Sintra

120,000

The number of birds that visit the Tagus estuary during migration season.

LISBON
OFF THE BEATEN TRACK

Lisbon is deservedly one of Europe's most popular destinations, meaning that queues for its major attractions are not uncommon. There is no need to travel far, however, to escape the crowds at these lesser-known gems in and around the city.

Lesser-Known Landmarks

Those who prefer crowd-free sights should head for the Aqueduto das Águas Livres (p146). Visitors can walk along the top of this historic aqueduct to take in dizzying views over the city. Also in the northern suburbs is the Palácio Fronteira (p146), a 17th-century palace and gardens famed for its sumptuous *azulejos*. A little further out is the Parque do Monteiro-Mor (p147), one of Lisbon's loveliest parks.

$\rightarrow$

Impressive arches of the Aqueduto das Águas Livres

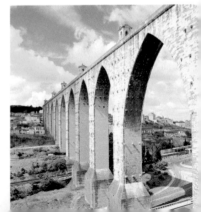

Escape the City

Sleepy Alcácer do Sal *(p169)*, whose hilltop castle overlooks the river Sado estuary, seems a world away from busy Lisbon. About an hour's drive south of the city centre, its charming lanes, pleasant waterside cafés and serene views from the 6th-century castle make this a perfect day trip destination. Or head further east to the riverside town of Carrasqueira *(p168)*, which sits alongside the Reserva Natural do Estuário do Tejo *(p163)*, an idyllic area known for its flamingos and other bird life.

←

Sunrise over Carrasqueira's harbour, and sleepy Alcácer do Sal *(inset)*

> 💬 INSIDER TIP
> ## A Coastal Retreat
>
> The Convento da Arrábida is a 16th-century monastery complex nestled in the hillside above the coast, less than 20 minutes by car from some of the region's best beaches. Head to Figueirinha or Galapos *(p168)* for soft sands sheltered from the Atlantic's breakers.

Seeking Sanctuary

Head further afield to find atmospheric religious sites. Not far from Belém's famous monuments lies the little-visited Ermida de São Jerónimo *(p126)*. This tiny chapel is one of Lisbon's earliest Manueline buildings, and affords fine views of the Tagus. The nearby Igreja da Memória is a handsome church and resting place for the Marquês de Pombal. In the hills above Sintra *(p152)* is the extraordinary 16th-century Convento dos Capuchos, where friars once lived in cork-lined cells, while south of Lisbon sits the beautiful Convento da Arrábida.

Verdant, moss-grown gardens of the Convento dos Capuchos ↑

A YEAR IN LISBON

JANUARY

△ **Epiphany** *(6 Jan)*. Celebrated by eating the traditional Epiphany cake, *bolo rei* (king's cake).

FEBRUARY

△ **Carnival** *(Shrove Tuesday, exact date varies)*. Spectacular parades with costumes and floats.

MAY

△ **Horse-Riding Exhibitions in Queluz** *(May–Oct)*. Demonstrations by the Portuguese Equestrian School in the palace gardens every Wednesday.
Sintra Music Festival *(last 3 weeks)*. Music and dance events are held throughout historic Sintra.

JUNE

Festas da Cidade *(throughout)*. A celebration of Lisbon, with highlights including a lively parade along the Avenida da Liberdade on 12 June, and the Santo António festival (12–13 Jun).
△ **Lisboa Pride** *(last weekend)*. A series of LGBT+ events take place across the capital, including a jubilant parade.

SEPTEMBER

△ **Avante!** *(1st weekend)*. A lively *festa* south of the Tagus that includes musical and literary events.
Nossa Senhora da Luz *(2nd weekend)*. A religious *festa* held near Sesimbra.

OCTOBER

Republic Day *(5 Oct)*. This public holiday commemorates the end of the monarchy in 1910 and the founding of the Portuguese republic.
△ **Rock 'n' Roll Lisbon Marathon** *(mid-Oct)*. The city's annual marathon, during which runners are accompanied by live bands as they race from Cascais to Lisbon's Parque das Nações.

MARCH

△ **Moda Lisboa** *(mid-Mar)*. Cutting-edge garments are on show at this, the first of two annual fashion weeks (the second takes place in October).
EDP Lisbon Half Marathon *(mid-Mar)*. Runners from all over the world participate in one of the capital's most popular sporting events.

APRIL

Peixe em Lisboa *(early–mid-Apr)*. Lisbon's annual fish festival in Parque Eduardo VII.
△ **Dia da Revoluçaõ** *(25 Apr)*. A public holiday to celebrate the Carnation Revolution in 1974 that ended 48 years of dictatorship.

JULY

△ **Nos Alive** *(early Jul)*. Big-name rock festival on the riverfront west of Belém, which has featured the likes of Arctic Monkeys and Snow Patrol.
Super Bock Super Rock *(3rd weekend)*. Local and international rock bands play at Parque das Nações.

AUGUST

Jazz em Agosto *(early Aug)*. Annual jazz festival in the gardens of the Museu Calouste Gulbenkian.
△ **Festival dos Oceanos** *(early Aug)*. A two-week cultural event including concerts and exhibitions.

NOVEMBER

All Saints' Day *(1 Nov)*. Candles are lit and flowers placed on graves to honour the dead.
△ **Dia de São Martinho** *(11 Nov)*. St Martin's Day, which celebrates the new chestnut season and the first tastings of the year's wine.

DECEMBER

Christmas *(24–25 Dec)*. The main celebration is a midnight Mass on 24 December, followed by a traditional meal of *bacalhau* (salted dried cod).
△ **New Year's Eve** *(31 Dec)*. A spectacular firework display takes place in Lisbon's Praça do Comércio to welcome the new year.

1

A BRIEF
HISTORY

Over the centuries, Lisbon has both flourished and suffered. Intrepid explorers in the 15th and 16th centuries made Portugal's capital a nexus of a global empire, only for the country to be beleaguered by invasions, revolutions and economic crises.

A New Port on the Tagus

In around 1200 BC, the Phoenicians founded a trading post on the banks of the Tagus river, at Allis Ubbo (calm harbour). From 205 BC, the settlement fell under Roman control, reaching the height of its importance when Julius Caesar became the governor in 60 BC. As the Roman Empire collapsed, the region declined at the hands of invading barbarian tribes from northern Europe. From AD 711, North African Moors occupied the peninsula, establishing Lisbon as an important trading hub.

Did You Know?

The Moorish legacy is still evident in Castelo de São Jorge and the streets of the Alfama district.

Timeline of events

1200 BC
Phoenicians found a trading post they call Allis Ubbo (calm harbour)

AD 711
Moorish invaders from North Africa colonize the city

1139
Afonso Henriques declares himself king of Portugal

1st Century BC
Romans establish Olisipo as the administrative capital of Lusitania

1147
Christian Crusaders evict the Moors from Lisbon under King Afonso Henriques

European Rule and the Age of Discovery

The first king of Portugal, Afonso Henriques, drove the Moors from Lisbon in 1147. Under Afonso, the Sé cathedral was built, and in 1256, the city was made the capital of Portugal, flourishing as a centre of culture. The university was founded in 1290 under Afonso's son, Dom Dinis, who also strengthened the city walls to help ward off any likely aggression from neighbouring Spain. Following the Battle of Aljubarrrota in 1385, peaceful relations with Spain allowed King João I to begin maritime explorations. In the 15th century, João's son Prince Henry the Navigator financed expeditions along the west coast of Africa, and in 1497, explorer Vasco da Gama set sail from Belém, becoming the first European to reach India by sea, and opening new trade routes between the continents. The resulting wealth from the spice trade made Lisbon the mercantile centre of Europe, and funded the construction of magnificent late-Gothic monuments by Manuel I (1495–1521). This era also saw the start of a reign of terror, with mass trials and executions perpetrated by the Inquisition, a Catholic movement that persecuted heretics and non-believers.

1 Historical map showing districts of Lisbon in 1840.

2 A painting portraying galleons from across Europe moored in Lisbon's harbour.

3 The cavernous interior of the Sé, which was originally built in the 12th century.

4 *Azulejos* depicting Henry the Navigator, who laid the foundations of Portugal's maritime expansion.

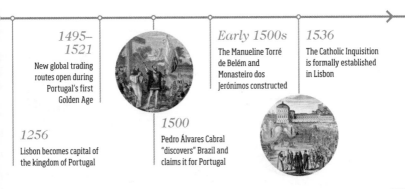

1495–1521

New global trading routes open during Portugal's first Golden Age

1256

Lisbon becomes capital of the kingdom of Portugal

1500

Pedro Álvares Cabral "discovers" Brazil and claims it for Portugal

Early 1500s

The Manueline Torré de Belém and Monasteiro dos Jerónimos constructed

1536

The Catholic Inquisition is formally established in Lisbon

Spanish Rule and New-Found Wealth

The young King Sebastião was killed at the battle of Alcácer-Quibrir in Morocco in 1578. In the absence of a direct heir, Sebastião's uncle – Philip II of Spain – assumed the throne, beginning a period of 60 years of Spanish rule, which lasted until 1640, when the Duke of Bragança was crowned João IV.

With the discovery of Brazilian gold in 1697, Lisbon enjoyed a new wave of prosperity. From 1706, João V began an ambitious building programme, which included the construction of the Águas Livres aqueduct, the fruits of which were devastated just a few years later when the great earthquake struck the city in 1755.

The 19th Century

The Portuguese royal family were forced to flee to Brazil in 1807 ahead of Napoleon's invading army, and Rio de Janeiro briefly became capital of the Portuguese empire. British generals Beresford and Wellington drove out Napoleon in 1811, but the royal family did not return to Portugal until 1821. In the late 19th century, a period of economic revival and industrialization saw vast expansion of the city's infrastructure.

THE GREAT EARTHQUAKE

The great earthquake of 1755 killed more than 10 per cent of Lisbon's population. It was so violent that shocks were felt as far away as Italy, and it had a profound effect on European thought – it was seen by some as an act of divine wrath. Responsibility for rebuilding the city fell to José I's chief minister, the Marquês de Pombal.

Timeline of events

1581
Philip II of Spain becomes Filipe I of Portugal after political manoeuvrings

1640
The Portuguese Duke of Bragança takes the throne

1811–21
Portugal becomes a quasi-British protectorate until João VI returns in 1821

1807–11
Napoleon's army invades, and the monarchy flees to Brazil

1910
Manuel II flees to Britain as Portugal is declared a republic

Salazar and the 20th Century

Republicanism had grown among the urban poor in the late 19th century, and in 1908, King Carlos was assassinated in Praça do Comércio. Two years later, a republic was declared in Praça do Município. There was little political stability until António Salazar's ruthless dictatorship, which lasted from 1932 to 1968, and saw Lisbon modernized at the expense of the rest of the country. In 1974, the largely peaceful Carnation Revolution finally ended Salazar's totalitarian regime.

Lisbon Today

Portuguese politics stabilized from 1986, after Portugal joined the European Communities. Investment flooded into Lisbon, with lucrative events hosted such as the 1998 Expo. The city saw a spate of new building, including the construction of the Ponte Vasco da Gama and the development of the Parque das Nações. Thanks to a boom in tourism, Lisbon has largely resisted the worst of the recession which affected much of Portugal after the economic crash of 2008. Today the capital is one of the most popular city-break destinations Europe.

1 Portrait of Felipe I (Philip II of Spain). ↑

2 Engraving showing the flooding that followed the 1755 earthquake.

3 Trams, introduced to Lisbon in 1873.

4 Vasco da Gama bridge, constructed in 1998.

Did You Know?

Lisbon's Ponte 25 de Abril was known as Ponte de Salazar until the Carnation Revolution.

1932–68
António Salazar rules as a ruthless dictator

1974
The right-wing regime is overthrown in the Carnation Revolution

1986
Portugal becomes a member of the European Communities

2007
The Lisbon Treaty is signed in Belém, forming the EU constitution

2018
A record number of tourists visit Lisbon

EXPERIENCE

The sleek ly curved Museu de Arte, Arquitetura e Tecnologia, Belém

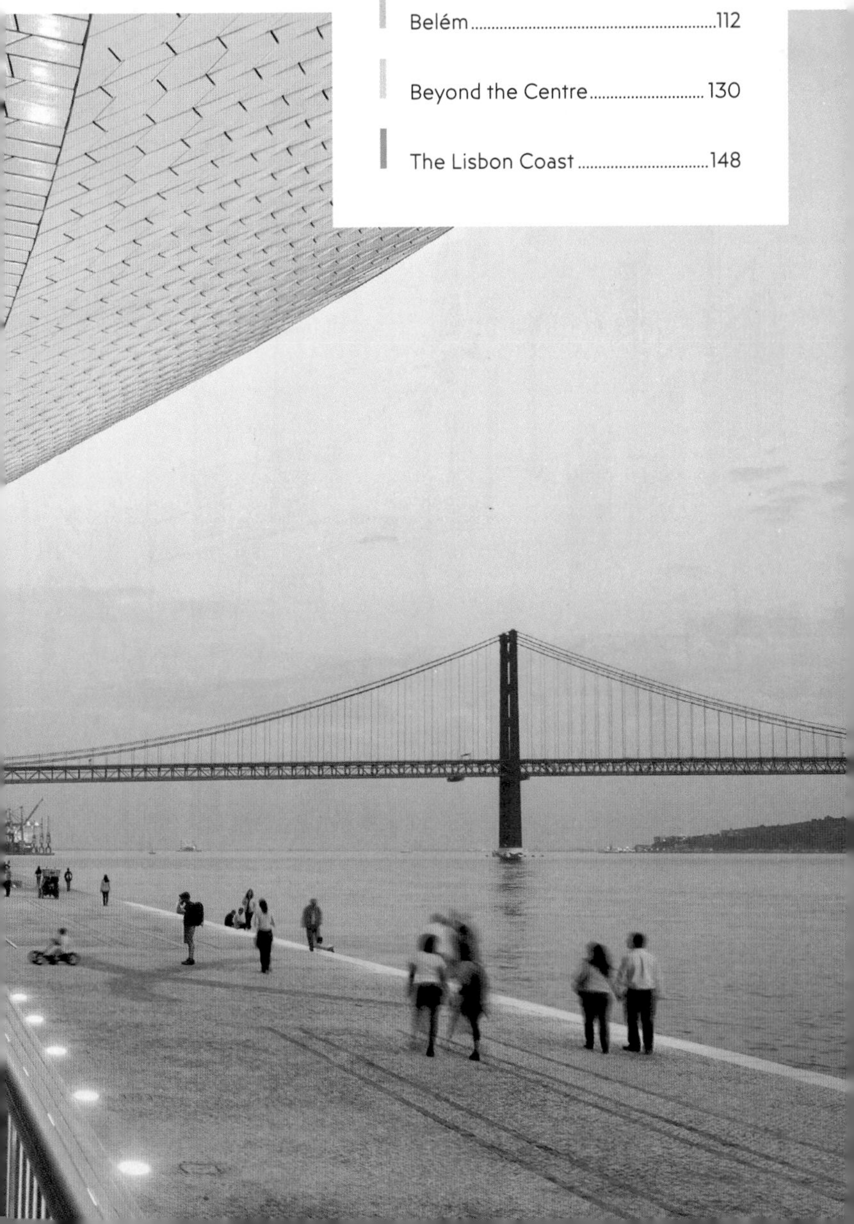

ALFAMA

It is difficult to believe that humble Alfama, the oldest and most atmospheric of Lisbon's neighbourhoods, was once the city's most desirable quarter. It was first settled by the Romans but flourished in Moorish times, when the tightly packed *becos* (alleyways) and tiny squares comprised the whole city. The Moors took advantage of Alfama's slopes, building the fortified Castelo de São Jorge on the crown of the hill and turning the city into a defensive stronghold.

But even that couldn't hold off crusaders forever. The city was captured by Afonso Henriques in 1147, and the seeds of Alfama's decline were sown in the Middle Ages when wealthy residents moved west for fear of earthquakes, leaving the quarter to fishermen and paupers. Many of its buildings survived the 1755 earthquake – although no Moorish houses still stand – and the quarter retains its kasbah-like layout. Compact houses line steep streets and stairways, their façades strung with washing, and daily life still revolves around local grocery stores and small, cellar-like taverns.

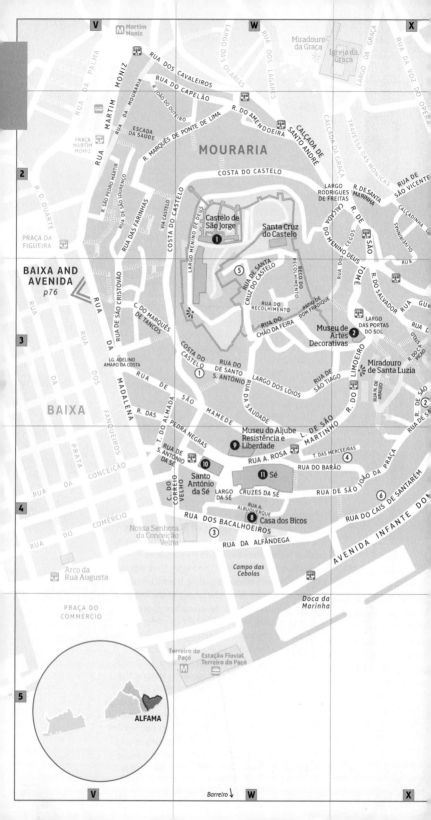

M Martim
Moniz

RUA DOS CAVALEIROS

RUA DO CAPELÃO

LARGO DAS OLARIAS

RUA DOS LAGARES

Miradouro
da Graça

Igreja da
Graça

RUA DA GRAÇA

RUA DA VOZ DO OPERA

RUA DA PALMA

RUA MARTIM MONIZ

RUA DA MOURARIA

R. JOÃO DO OUTEIRO

ESCADA
DA SAÚDE

R. MARQUÊS DE PONTE DE LIMA

PRAÇA
MARTIM
MONIZ

R. DO AMENDOEIRA

CALÇADA DE
SANTO ANDRÉ

CALÇADA DA GRAÇA

TRAVESSA DAS MÓNICAS

RUA DE
SÃO VICENTE

MOURARIA

COSTA DO CASTELO

LARGO
RODRIGUES
DE FREITAS

R. DE SANTA
MARINHA

CALÇADINHA

R. D. DUARTE

R. SÃO PEDRO MARTIR

RUA DE SÃO LOURENÇO

RUA DAS FARINHAS

VIA CASTELO

COSTA DO CASTELO

CALÇADA
DO MENINO DE DEUS

R. DE
SÃO
VICENTE

OLIVEIRINHAS

2

PRAÇA DA
FIGUEIRA

Castelo de
São Jorge
1

Santa Cruz
do Castelo

LARGO MENINO DE DEUS

5

RUA DE SANTA
CRUZ DO CASTELO

BECO DO
RECOLHIMENTO

RUA DOS CEGOS

RUA DE
SÃO TOMÉ

R. DO SALVADOR

RUA GU

BAIXA AND
AVENIDA
p76

RUA DA

RUA DE SÃO CRISTOVÃO

C. DO MARQUÊS
DE TANCOS

RUA DO
CHÃO DA FEIRA

RUA DO
RECOLHIMENTO

RUA DE
SANTO
ANTÓNIO

PÁTIO DE
DOM FRADIQUE

Museu de
Artes
Decorativas **2**

LARGO
DAS PORTAS
DO SOL

RUA L

3

LG. ADELINO
AMARO DA COSTA

COSTA DO
CASTELO **1**

RUA DO
DE SANTO
S. ANTÓNIO

LARGO DOS LOIOS

RUA DE
SÃO TIAGO

Miradouro
de Santa Luzia

RUA DA SAUDADE

RUA DE
SÃO JOÃO
DO
LIMOEIRO

RUA N. DE
ARAUJO

RUA R. DE SÉ

2

R. DE SÉ

BAIXA

RUA DE
SÃO MAMEDE

L. DE SÃO
MARTINHO

R. DAS

RUA DO

MADALENA

R. DAS
PEDRA NEGRAS

Museu do Aljube
Resistência e
Liberdade **9**

T. DAS MERCEEIRAS **4**

RUA A. ROSA

RUA DO BARÃO

RUA DE
S. ANTÓNIO
DA SÉ

10

Santo
António
da Sé

LARGO
DA SÉ

11 Sé

CRUZES DA SÉ

RUA DE SÃO JOÃO DA PRAÇA

RUA DO CAIS DE SANTARÉM **6**

RUA DA

PRATA

CONCEIÇÃO

C. DO
CORREIO
VELHO

RUA A.
ALBUQUERQUE
8 Casa dos Bicos

AVENIDA INFANTE DO

FANQUEIROS

4

COMÉRCIO

Nossa Senhora
da Conceição
Velha

RUA DOS BACALHOEIROS
3

RUA DA ALFÂNDEGA

RUA
DO

Arco da
Rua Augusta

Campo das
Cebolas

*Doca da
Marinha*

PRAÇA DO
COMMERCIO

Terreiro do
Paço
M

Estação Fluvial
Terreiro do Paço

5

ALFAMA

ALFAMA

Must See

1. Castelo de São Jorge

Experience More

2. Museu de Artes Decorativas
3. São Vicente de Fora
4. Feira da Ladra
5. Santa Engrácia
6. Museu do Fado
7. Museu Militar
8. Casa dos Bicos
9. Museu do Aljube – Resistência e Liberdade
10. Santo António da Sé
11. Sé

Eat

1. Chapitô à Mesa
2. A Baiuca
3. Cantina Zé Avillez

Stay

4. Memmo Alfama
5. Solar do Castelo
6. Palacete Chafariz del Rei

❶ 🗺️ Ⓜ️ 🍴 🖥️ 🛍️

CASTELO DE SÃO JORGE

Torre de Ulisses

📍W2 🏛️Porta de São Jorge (entrance on Rua de Santa Cruz do Castelo) 🚌737 🚋28 ⏰Mar-Oct: 9am-9pm daily; Nov-Feb: 9am-6pm daily (check website for further details) 🌐castelodesaojorge.pt

Towering above central Lisbon, this Moorish citadel is one of the city's most recognizable landmarks. Though much of the present castle dates from a 1930s restoration, visitors still flock to the top of the hill to seek out traces of the city's history and enjoy the spectacular views laid out below.

Following the recapture of Lisbon from the Moors in 1147, Dom Afonso Henriques transformed their hilltop citadel into the residence of the Portuguese kings. In 1511, Manuel I built a more lavish palace in what is now the Praça do Comércio and the citadel castle was used variously as a theatre, prison and arms depot. After the 1755 earthquake, the ramparts remained in ruins until 1938, when António Salazar *(p55)* began a complete renovation, rebuilding the "medieval" walls and adding gardens and wildfowl. The castle may not be authentic, but the gardens and the narrow streets of the Santa Cruz district within the walls make a pleasant stroll, and views from the observation terrace are some of the finest in Lisbon. Other attractions on-site include the city's only camera obscura and the Casa do Leão restaurant, built within part of the former royal residence. Book a table for dinner; the restaurant is also open at lunchtime to those with a ticket for the castle.

The Museu do Castelo, which displays artifacts from the archaeological site and charts the history of the city.

1️⃣ The citadel is set on a hilltop location above Lisbon's colourful rooftops.

2️⃣ Visitors can climb the towers and walk along the reconstructed ramparts of the castle walls.

3️⃣ The castle's Observation Terrace is a large shaded square offering spectacular views over the city.

Porta de Martim Moniz, a gate named after the knight who gave his life to keep it open for Afonso Henriques' troops in 1147.

An archaeological site containing the ruins of settlements dating from before the original citadel was built.

The 12th-century church of Santa Cruz do Castelo, inside which is a 17th-century statue of St George.

← The tangled site of the Castelo São Jorge, packed inside a walled perimeter

Rua de Santa Cruz do Castelo, a pretty street south of the castle.

Porta de São Jorge

Entrance

TORRE DE ULISSES

Named after the Greek hero Ulysses, who supposedly founded Lisbon on his meander home from Troy, this tower contains a camera obscura – a complicated system of lenses and mirrors that projects 360° views of the city onto the walls in real time. Views are weather-dependent; sunny mornings, when the light is soft, yield the clearest images.

→ Afonso Henriques, the first king of Portugal

EXPERIENCE MORE

2

Museu de Artes Decorativas

📍X3 🏛Largo das Portas do Sol 2 🚌737 🚃12, 28 🕐10am–5pm Wed–Mon 🚫1 Jan, 1 May, 25 Dec 🌐fress.pt

Also known as the Ricardo do Espírito Santo Silva Foundation, the museum was set up in 1953 to preserve the traditions and increase public awareness of the Portuguese decorative arts. The foundation was named after a banker who bought the 17th-century Palácio Azurara in 1947 to house his fine collection of furniture, textiles, silver and ceramics. Among the 17th- and 18th-century antiques displayed in this handsome four-storey mansion are many fine pieces in exotic woods, including an 18th-century rosewood backgammon and chess table. Also of note are the collections of 18th-century silver and Chinese porcelain, and hand-embroidered wool carpets from Arraiolos. The spacious rooms still retain some original ceilings and azulejo panels.

In the adjoining building are workshops where artisans preserve the techniques of cabinet-making, gilding, book-binding, wood-carving and other traditional crafts. Temporary exhibitions, lectures and concerts are also held in the museum.

3

São Vicente de Fora

📍Y2 🏛Largo de São Vicente 📞218 885 652 🚌712, 734 🚃28 🕐9am–5pm Tue–Sat, 9–11am Sun; museum: 10am–5pm Tue–Sun 🚫Public hols

St Vincent was proclaimed Lisbon's patron saint in 1173, when his relics were transferred from the Algarve to a church on this site outside (fora) the city walls. Designed by the Italian architect Filippo Terzi, and completed in 1627, the sober off-white façade is in Italian Renaissance style, with towers either side and three arches leading to the entrance hall. Statues of saints Augustine, Sebastian and Vincent can be seen over the entrance. The adjoining former Augustinian monastery, reached via the nave, retains its 16th-century cistern and vestiges of the former cloister, but it is visited mainly for its 18th-century azulejos. Among the panels in the entrance hall off the first cloister there are lively, though historically

→

Intricate marble inlays adorning São Vicente de Fora

inaccurate, tile scenes of Afonso Henriques attacking Lisbon and Santarém. Deeper into the monastery, floral designs and cherubs illustrate the fables of La Fontaine. A passageway leads behind the church to the old refectory, transformed into the Bragança Pantheon in 1885. The stone sarcophagi of almost every king and queen are here, from João IV, who died in 1656, to Manuel II, last king of Portugal. Only Maria I and Pedro IV are not buried here. A stone mourner kneels at the tomb of Carlos I and his son Luís Felipe, assassinated in Praça do Comércio in 1908. The church now operates as a museum, with access to the Bragança Pantheon.

4

Feira da Ladra

📍Y2 🏛Campo de Santa Clara 🚌712 🚃28 🕐9am–5pm Tue & Sat

The stalls of the so-called "Thieves' Market" have

↑ Ornate carriage on display at Museu de Artes Decorativas

occupied this site on the edge of the Alfama for over a century, laid out under the shade of trees or canopies. As the fame of this flea market has grown, bargains are increasingly hard to find among the mass of bric-a-brac, but a few of the vendors have interesting wrought-iron work, prints and tiles, as well as second-hand clothes. Evidence of Portugal's colonial past is reflected in the stalls selling African statuary, masks and jewellery.

←

A bric-a-brac stall at the Feira da Ladra flea market

5

Santa Engrácia

📍 Y2 🏛 Campo de Santa Clara 📞 218 854 820 🚌 712 🚋 28 🕐 10am–6pm Tue-Sun (to 5pm Nov-Mar) 🚫 1 Jan, 25 Apr, Easter Sun, 13 Jun, 24 & 25 Dec

One of Lisbon's most striking landmarks, the soaring dome of Santa Engrácia (officially known as Panteão Nacional) punctuates the skyline in the east of the city. The original church collapsed in a storm in 1681. The first stone of the new Baroque monument, laid in 1682, marked the beginning of a 284-year saga that led to the invention of a saying that a Santa Engrácia job was never done. The church was not completed until 1966.

The interior is paved with coloured marble and crowned by a giant cupola. As the

GREAT VIEW
Miradouro de Santa Luzia

The terrace by the church of Santa Luzia provides a sweeping view over the Alfama and the Tagus river. Landmarks, from left to right, are the cupola of Santa Engrácia, the church of Santo Estêvão and the white towers of São Miguel. While tourists admire the views, old men play cards under the bougainvillea-clad pergola.

National Pantheon, it houses cenotaphs of Portuguese heroes, such as Vasco da Gama (p122) and Afonso de Albuquerque, Viceroy of India (1502–15) on the left, and on the right Henry the Navigator (p53). More contemporary tombs include that of the fadista Amália Rodrigues (p43). A lift up to the dome offers a magnificent 360-degree panorama of the city.

↑ José Malhoa's *O Fado*, a haunting portrait hanging at the Museu do Fado

arms depot, visits here begin in the Vasco da Gama Room, with cannons and modern murals depicting the discovery of the sea route to India. The Salas da Grande Guerra display exhibits related to World War I. Other rooms focus on the evolution of weapons in Portugal, from flints to spears to rifles. The courtyard, flanked by cannons, tells the story of Portugal in tiled panels, from the Christian reconquest to World War I. The Portuguese artillery section displays the wagon used to transport the triumphal arch to Rua Augusta (*p88*).

6

Museu do Fado

📍Y3 🏠Largo do Chafariz de Dentro 1 🚌728, 735, 759, 794 🕐10am–6pm Tue–Sun 🌐museudofado.pt

Alfama is considered the true home of *fado* (*p42*) and this museum portrays the influence that this ever-popular and intensely heartfelt genre of music has had on the city over the past two centuries. A permanent display traces the genre's history from its origins in the early 19th century to the present day, from Maria Severa, the first *fado* diva, to more contemporary singers like Amália Rodrigues and Mariza. Regular temporary exhibitions take place during the year on a range of musical themes, along with the occasional live *fado* concert.

7

Museu Militar

📍Y3 🏠Largo do Museu da Artilharia 🚌728, 735, 759 🚋28 🕐10am–5pm Tue–Sun 🚫Public hols 🌐exercito.pt

Located on the site of a 16th-century cannon foundry and

8

Casa dos Bicos

📍W4 🏠Rua dos Bacalhoeiros 10 📞218 802 040 🚌728, 735, 759 🚋15, 25 🕐10am–6pm Mon–Sat

Faced with diamond-shaped stones (*bicos*), Casa dos Bicos (House of Spikes) looks rather conspicuous among all the other

---

⛰ GREAT VIEW
Miradouro da Graça

North of Alfama, the suburb of Graça is visited chiefly for the vistas from its *miradouro* (viewpoint). The panorama of rooftops and skyscrapers is less spectacular than the view from the Castelo de São Jorge, but it is a popular spot, particularly in the early evenings, when couples sit at café tables under the pines.

Monumental portico at the entrance to the Museu Militar ↑

↑ Street café in front of the 16th-century Casa dos Bicos

buildings in the Alfama area. It was built in 1523 for Brás de Albuquerque, illegitimate son of Afonso, Viceroy of India and conqueror of Goa and Malacca. The façade is an adaptation of a style that was popular across Europe during the 16th century. The top two storeys, ruined in the earthquake of 1755, were restored in the 1980s, recreating the original from old views of Lisbon in tile panels and engravings. In the interim the building was used for salting fish (Rua dos Bacalhoeiros means "street of the cod fishermen").

Following an extensive renovation in the 20th century, Casa dos Bicos now plays host to the headquarters of the José Saramago Foundation. It is also home to a permanent exhibition dedicated to the life and works of this Nobel Prize-winning author, who died in 2010. A variety of cultural events often take place here; these include concerts, plays and book releases, along with a range of seminars, debates and lively talks.

9 ⊡

Museu do Aljube – Resistência e Liberdade

🅠 W4 🏠 Rua Augusta Rosa 42 🕒 10am-6pm Tue-Sat 🗓 1 Jan, 1 May, 25 Dec 🅦 museudoaljube.pt

This fascinating museum was once used by António Salazar – who ruled Portugal as a dictator from 1926 until the revolution of 1974 – to imprison his political opponents. It is dedicated to those who were prepared to fight for democracy, both in Portugal and in its former colonies. Three floors are filled with evocative photos, posters and radio broadcasts, with labelling in English. There are also harrowing personal accounts from people who were incarcerated and often tortured for views that were considered contrary to those of the state; many of these inmates were later deported to Madeira or the Azores. Their cramped, windowless cells can still be visited.

The basement houses archaeological finds from beneath the building, which date back to Moorish times, while the top-floor café offers fine views over the river.

Lisbon's colourful skyline seen from the Miradouro da Graça viewpoint

10 ⟨⟩

Santo António da Sé

📍W4 🏛Largo Santo
António da Sé, 24 🚍218
869145 🚌737 🚊12, 28
🕐8am–7pm daily (to
8pm Sat & Sun); Museu
Antoniano: 10am–6pm
Tue–Sun

The popular little church of Santo António allegedly stands on the site of the house in which St Anthony was born. The crypt, reached via the tiled sacristy on the left of the church, is all that remains of the original church destroyed by the earthquake of 1755. Work began on the new church in 1757 headed by Mateus Vicente, architect of the Basílica da Estrela (p106), and was partially funded by donations collected by local children with the cry "a small coin for St Anthony". Even today the floor of the tiny chapel in the crypt is strewn with euros and the walls are scrawled with devotional messages from worshippers.

The church's façade blends the undulating curves of the Baroque style with Neo-Classical Ionic columns on either side of the main portal. Inside, on the way down to the crypt, a modern azulejo panel commemorates the visit of Pope John Paul II in 1982. In 1995 the church was given a facelift for the saint's eighth centenary. It is traditional for young couples to visit the church on their wedding day and leave flowers for St Anthony, who is believed to bring good luck to new marriages. Next door, in the building thought to be where St Anthony was born, the small Museu Antoniano houses artifacts relating to the saint, along with gold- and silverware that used to decorate the church. The most charming exhibit is a 17th-century tiled panel of St Anthony preaching to the fish.

↑ The impressive
Baroque-façade of
Santo António da Sé

11 ⟨⟩

Sé

📍W4 🏛Largo da Sé 🚍218
866752 🚌737 🚊12, 28
🕐9am–7pm daily (to 5pm
Mon & Sun); treasury:
10am–5pm Mon–Sat

In 1150, three years after Afonso Henriques recaptured Lisbon from the Moors, he built a cathedral for the first bishop of Lisbon, the English Crusader Gilbert of Hastings, on the site of the old mosque. Sé is short for Sede Episcopal, the seat (or see) of a bishop. Devastated by three earth tremors in the 14th century, as well as the earthquake of 1755, and renovated over the centuries, the cathedral you see today blends a variety of architectural styles. The façade, with twin castellated bell towers and a splendid rose window, retains its solid Romanesque aspect. The gloomy interior is simple and austere, and little remains of the embellishment lavished upon it by King João V in the first half of the 18th century. Beyond the reno-vated Romanesque nave, the ambulatory has nine

---

SANTO ANTÓNIO (C 1195-1231)

The best-loved saint of the Lisboetas is St Antony of Padua. Although born and raised in Lisbon, he spent the last months of his life in Padua, Italy. St Anthony joined the Franciscan Order in 1220, impressed by some crusading friars he had met at Coimbra. The friar was a learned and passionate preacher, known for his devotion to the poor and his ability to convert heretics. Many statues and paintings of St Anthony depict him carrying the infant Jesus on a book, while others show him preaching to fish, as St Francis preached to birds. In 1934 Pope Pius XI declared St Anthony a patron saint of Portugal.

EXPERIENCE Alfama

Gothic chapels. The Capela de Santo Ildefonso contains the 14th-century sarcophagi of Lopo Fernandes Pacheco, companion in arms to King Afonso IV, and his wife, Maria Vilalobos. The bearded figure of the nobleman, who is holding a sword in his hand, and his wife, clutching a prayer book, are carved onto the tombs with their dogs sitting faithfully at their feet. In the adjacent chancel are the tombs of Afonso IV and his wife, Dona Beatriz.

The Gothic cloister (closed for renovation until 2020) has elegant double arches with some finely carved capitals. One of the chapels is still fitted with its 13th-century wrought-iron gate. Ongoing archaeological excavations in the cloister have unearthed various Roman and other remains.

To the left of the cathedral entrance the Franciscan chapel contains the font where St Anthony was baptized in 1195 and is decorated with a tiled scene of him preaching to the fish. The adjacent chapel contains a Baroque Nativity scene made of cork, wood and terracotta by Machado de Castro (1766).

The treasury is at the top of the staircase on the right. It houses silver, ecclesiastical robes, statuary, illustrated manuscripts and a few relics associated with St Vincent, which were transferred to Lisbon from Cabo de São Vicente in southern Portugal in 1173. Legend has it that two sacred ravens kept a vigil over the boat that transported the relics. The ravens and the boat became a symbol of the city of Lisbon, still very much in use today. It is also said that the ravens' descendants used to dwell in the cloisters of the cathedral.

Interior of the city's cathedral, adorned with stunning stained-glass *(inset)* ↓

A SHORT WALK

ALFAMA

Distance 600 m (0.4 miles) **Nearest station** Graça bus stop
Time 15 minutes

A fascinating quarter at any time of day, the Alfama comes to life in the late afternoon and early evening; time your walk for this hour, when the locals emerge at their doorways and the small taverns start to fill. Given the steep streets and steps of the neighbourhood, the least strenuous approach is to start at the top and work your way down. A wander through the maze of winding alleyways will reveal picturesque corners and crumbling churches, plus panoramic views from shady terraces, such as the Miradouro de Santa Luzia. A new generation of younger residents has also resulted in a small number of trendy shops and bars.

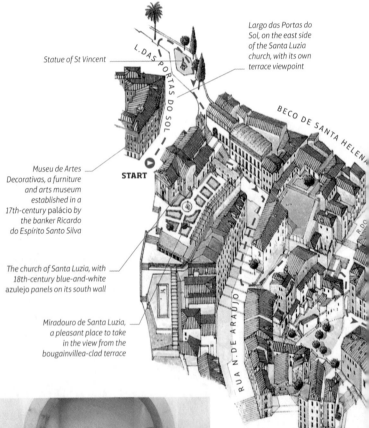

Statue of St Vincent

Largo das Portas do Sol, on the east side of the Santa Luzia church, with its own terrace viewpoint

L. DAS PORTAS DO SOL

BECO DE SANTA HELENA

START

Museu de Artes Decorativas, a furniture and arts museum established in a 17th-century palácio by the banker Ricardo do Espírito Santo Silva

The church of Santa Luzia, with 18th-century blue-and-white azulejo panels on its south wall

Miradouro de Santa Luzia, a pleasant place to take in the view from the bougainvillea-clad terrace

RUA N. DE ARAÚJO

← An azulejo-lined staircase at the Museu de Artes Decorativas

↑ The spectacular cityscape, as seen from the Miradouro de Santa Luzia

Locator Map
For more detail see p60

Beco das Cruzes is a steep cobbled street, above which locals often string their washing between the tightly packed houses.

Restaurants, hidden in a labyrinth of alleyways, spill out onto open-air patios.

The church of Nossa Senhora dos Remédios, whose pinnacled Manueline portal is all that remains of the original building.

BECO DAS CRUZES

RUA DE SÃO MIGUEL

BECO DO MEXIAS

LARGO DO CHAFARIZ DE DENTRO

BECO DO POCINHO

RUA DE SÃO PEDRO

Rua de São Pedro, where a lively early-morning fish market is held daily

Largo do Chafariz de Dentro, a square named after the 17th-century fountain (chafariz) that was originally placed within (dentro) rather than outside the 14th-century city walls

FINISH

São Miguel was rebuilt after the 1755 earthquake, although it retains a few earlier features.

0 metres   25   N
0 yards   25   ↑

A LONG WALK

BAIXA, ALFAMA, CASTELO AND MOURARIA

Distance: 3 km (2 miles) **Walking time:** 60 minutes **Nearest Station:** Praça do Comércio tram stop **Difficulty:** Steep in places, with steps

From the late-18th-century splendour of the Baixa, this walk takes you into the winding alleyways of Alfama, a much older and humbler neighbourhood. Castelo de São Jorge crowns the hill, standing on a site that has been fortified for thousands of years. Behind it, Mouraria was the quarter to which Lisbon's remaining Moors were relegated in 1147. Their legacy is believed to survive most notably in the cadences of *fado*, which is at its most authentic here.

Rua de São Lourenço is the heart of Mouraria, an area that is a warren of streets and steps.

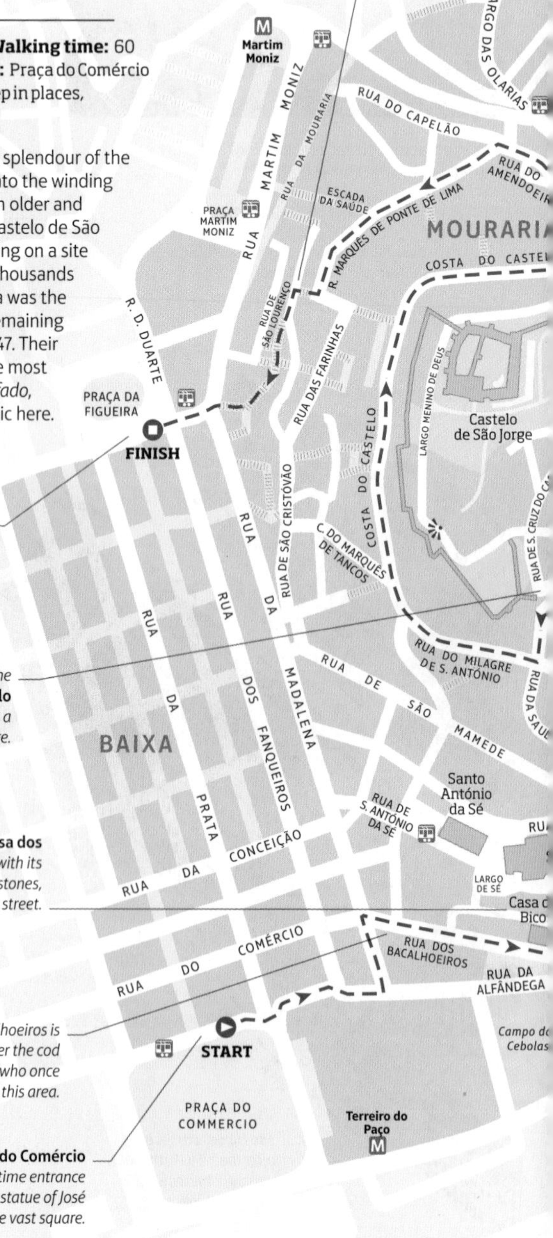

*End the walk at **Praça da Figueira** (p88), which has an impressive bronze equestrian statue of João I.*

*In a niche inside the gateway to the **Castelo de São Jorge** (p62) is a statue of St George.*

*The unmistakable **Casa dos Bicos** (p66) with its diamond-shaped stones, stands out on this street.*

Rua dos Bacalhoeiros is named after the cod merchants who once dominated this area.

*Begin the walk at **Praça do Comércio** (p80), once the grand maritime entrance to Lisbon. Admire the large statue of José I at the centre of the vast square.*

MOURARIA

Castelo de São Jorge

BAIXA

Santo António da Sé

Casa dos Bicos

FINISH

START

PRAÇA DO COMERCIO

Terreiro do Paço

Locator Map
For more detail see p60 and p78

According to legend, the knight Martim Moniz prevented the gate from closing with his own body, sacrificing his life to allow Afonso Henriques and his men to storm the castle.

Largo das Portas do Sol has a statue of the city's patron saint, São Vicente. Across the square is the **Museu de Artes Decorativas** *(p64).*

The panorama seen from the Santo Estêvão church is one of Lisbon's finest views.

The stalls selling fresh fish along Rua de São Pedro are an Alfama institution.

Museu de Artes Decorativas

Santo Estêvão Church

ALFAMA

Museu do Fado

Pois Café

Pois Café, near the Sé, has a cosy vaulted living room, perfect for a coffee break.

0 metres 150
0 yards 150
N ↑

↑ A typical Lisbon tram trundling past historic Sé cathedral

BAIXA AND AVENIDA

It was the Baixa that felt the full force of the 1755 earthquake, which destroyed much of the neighbourhood. From its ruins, the Marquês de Pombal created an entirely new centre, using a grid layout of streets and linking the riverfront Praça do Comércio with the busy Rossio square. The streets were flanked by uniform, Neo-Classical buildings and named according to the shopkeepers and craftsmen who traded there – Rua do Ouro was the goldsmiths' street, and Rua dos Sapateiros that of the shoemakers.

Some 80 years later, the Arco da Rua Augusta was built to celebrate the Baixa's reconstruction. The Avenida de Liberdade followed shortly afterwards, laid out in 1882 as the city's main avenue between the Baixa and Parque Eduardo VII. Fashioned on Paris's Champs-Élysées, it is still the city's most upmarket area, lined with grand 19th-century mansions and a tree-dotted central strip.

BAIXA AND AVENIDA

Must Sees
1 Praça do Comércio
2 Elevador de Santa Justa

Experience More
3 Jardim Botânico
4 Praça dos Restauradores
5 Avenida da Liberdade
6 Casa Museu Medeiros e Almeida
7 Rossio
8 Rua Augusta
9 Praça da Figueira
10 Museu da Sociedade de Geografia
11 Núcleo Arqueológico
12 MUDE (Museu do Design e da Moda)
13 Nossa Senhora da Conceição Velha

Eat
① Bonjardim, Rei dos Frangos
② Cervejaria Ribadouro
③ Confeitaria Nacional

Stay
④ Hotel Heritage Avenida Liberdade
⑤ Hotel Almalusa
⑥ Inspira Santa Marta

Shop
⑦ Manuel Tavares
⑧ Madeira House

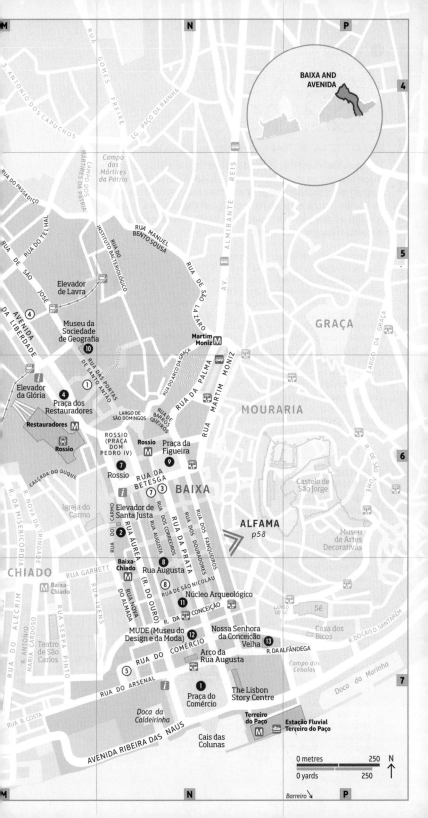

① 🍴 ☕ 🛍️

PRAÇA DO COMÉRCIO

📍 N7   🚌 711, 714, 759, 794 & many other routes   🚋 15, 18, 25

The beautiful riverfront Praça do Comércio is a vast square with shady arcades on three sides and the wide expanse of the Tagus lapping at its southern edge. It was the centrepiece of the Marquês de Pombal's post-earthquake redesign of the city, and today remains a lively gathering place that hosts cultural events and festivals throughout the year.

Known to locals as *Terreiro do Paço* (Palace Square), this huge open space was the site of the royal palace for 400 years. Manuel I transferred the royal residence from Castelo de São Jorge to this more convenient spot by the river in 1511. When the original palace was destroyed in the 1755 earthquake, Pombal housed the new palace in spacious arcaded buildings around three sides of the square. On the fourth side, grand marble steps stretch down to the water's edge.

Highlights of the square include a huge bronze statue of King José I, the impressive Arco da Rua Augusta on the north side and the Lisbon Story Centre, an interactive museum exploring events in the city's history.

HISTORY IN THE MAKING

The Praça do Comércio has been the scene of major events throughout Lisbon's history. On 1 February 1908, King Carlos and his son Luís Felipe were assassinated as they passed through the square, an event that eventually led to the abolition of the monarchy and declaration of the Republic two years later. Then in 1974, the square saw the first uprising of the Armed Forces Movement, whose soldiers - sporting carnations in their rifles - overthrew the Caetano regime in a bloodless revolution.

1 Locals gather on the square's stone steps leading down to the wide Tagus river.

2 Museum-goers take in an unusual exhibit at the Lisbon Story Centre.

3 The colonnade and archways around the square's edges provide a cool place to stroll.

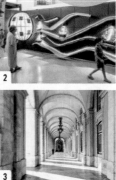

Did You Know?

The Martinho da Arcada, set in a corner of the square, is Lisbon's oldest café.

VIRTVTIBVS
MAIORVM
VT SIT OMNIBVS.DOCVMENTO. P P D.

↑ Bustling Praça do Comércio, dominated by a huge statue of King José I

Lisbon's historic centre unfurling beneath the viewing gallery at the top of the lift ↑

Did You Know?

The Santa Justa is the only remaining vertical street lift in the city.

2 ✎

ELEVADOR DE SANTA JUSTA

📍N6 🏠Rua de Santa Justa and Largo do Carmo
📞213 613 000 🕐7:30am-9:30pm daily (to 11pm May-Sep)

Sandwiched between pale stone buildings, this arresting iron structure is a vertical link between Lisbon's lowest and highest neighbourhoods. A platform at the top provides spectacular city views.

Also known as the Elevador do Carmo, this Neo-Gothic lift was built at the turn of the 20th century by French architect Raoul Mesnier du Ponsard, a student of Alexandre Gustave Eiffel. Made of iron and embellished with filigree, it is one of the more eccentric features of the Baixa. The ticket office is located at the foot of the lift, and from here passengers can travel up and down inside the tower in one of two smart, wood-panelled cabins with brass fittings. At the top is a walkway linking the Baixa with Largo do Carmo in the Bairro Alto, 32 m (105 ft) above. The apex of the tower, reached via an extremely tight spiral stairway, is given over to a viewing gallery. This high vantage point commands splendid views of Rossio, the Baixa, the castle on the opposite hill, the river and the nearby ruins of the Carmo church. The fire that gutted the Chiado district (p101) was extinguished close to the lift.

A stunning panorama of the Baixa's grid pattern can be seen from the platform.

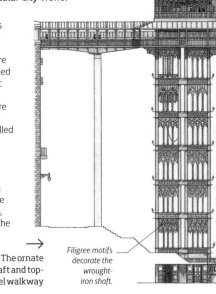

→ The ornate lift shaft and top-level walkway

Filigree motifs decorate the wrought-iron shaft.

EXPERIENCE MORE

Jardim Botânico

📍L5 🏛Rua da Escola Politécnica 58-60 🚌758 Ⓜ Rato 🕐Gardens: 9am-8pm daily (to 5pm Oct-Mar); MUHNAC: 10am-5pm Tue-Fri, 11am-6pm Sat & Sun 🔒Public hols 🌐museus.ulisboa.pt

This complex comprises a museum and 4 ha (10 acres) of gardens. The botanical gardens are well kept, and it is worth paying the entrance fee to wander among the exotic trees and dense paths as the gardens descend from the main entrance towards Rua da Alegria. A magnificent, verdant avenue of lofty palms connects the two levels.

The Museu Nacional de História Natural e da Ciência, or MUHNAC (National Museum of Natural History and Science), has collections on botany, zoology, anthropology, geology and palaeontology, as well as hosting temporary exhibitions on themes such as dinosaurs. The museum also exhibits scientific instruments dating from the 16th to the 20th century and holds popular, child-friendly programmes that demonstrate basic scientific principles.

↑ Steps leading up to the impressive Elevador de Santa Justa

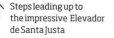

💬 INSIDER TIP
Upwardly Mobile

The Santa Justa lift is technically part of Lisbon's public transport system – and therefore a ride is covered by the 24-hour public transport tickets that can be purchased from any metro station *(p177)*.

↑ Shaded path descending among exotic foliage, Jardim Botânico

④
Praça dos Restauradores

🚇 M6 🚌 709, 711, 736 & many other routes
Ⓜ Restauradores

This square, distinguished by its soaring obelisk erected in 1886, commemorates Portugal's liberation from the Spanish yoke in 1640. The bronze figures on the pedestal depict Victory, holding a palm and a crown, and Freedom. The names and dates that are inscribed on the sides of the obelisk are those of the battles of the War of Restoration.

On the west side, the Palácio Foz now houses a tourist office and other businesses. It was built by Francesco Savario Fabri in 1755–77 for the Marquês de Castelo-Melhor and renamed after the Marquês de Foz, who lived here in the 19th century. The smart Avenida Palace Hotel, on the southwest side of the square, was designed by José Luís Monteiro (1848–1942), who also built Rossio railway station.

⑤
Avenida da Liberdade

🚇 M5 🚌 709, 711, 736 & many other routes
Ⓜ Restauradores, Avenida

After the earthquake of 1755, the Marquês de Pombal created the Passeio Público (public promenade) in the area now occupied by the lower part of Avenida da Liberdade and Praça dos Restauradores. Despite its name, enjoyment of the park was restricted to Lisbon's high society and walls and gates ensured the exclusion of the lower classes. In 1821, when the Liberals came to power, the barriers were pulled down and the Avenida and square became open to all.

The Avenida da Liberdade you see today was built in 1879–82 to replicate the sophistication and style of the Champs-Elysées in Paris. The wide tree-lined avenue became a focus for pageants, festivities and demonstrations. A war memorial stands as a tribute to those who died in World War I. The avenue still retains a certain elegance, with fountains and café tables shaded by trees; however, it no longer makes for a peaceful stroll. The once majestic thoroughfare, 90 m (295 ft) wide and decorated with abstract pavement patterns, is now divided by seven lanes of traffic linking Praça dos Restauradores and Praça Marquês de Pombal to the north. Many of the Art Nouveau façades have given way to modern ones occupied by offices, hotels or shopping complexes, though some of the original mansions have been preserved. Look out for the Neo-Classical Tivoli cinema at No 188, with an original 1920s kiosk outside, and Casa Lambertini with its colourful mosaic decoration at No 166.

> **Did You Know?**
>
> Rossio is home to a public mirror engraved with the words "correct your tie's knot here".

> The Avenida da Liberdade you see today was built in 1879-82 to replicate the sophistication and style of the Champs-Elysées in Paris.

The soaring obelisk dominating Praça dos Restauradores ↑

↑ Rossio, featuring wavy paving and a fountain *(inset)* that is illuminated at night

6

Casa Museu Medeiros e Almeida

📍 L5 🏠 Rua Rosa Araújo 41
🕐 10am–5pm Mon–Sat
🌐 casa-museumedeirose almeida.pt

This little-known museum off the Avenida is in the former home of António Medeiros e Almeida, an industrialist who amassed an astonishing collection of international arts and crafts before bequeathing it to the nation in the 1970s.

Today the collection sprawls across 27 galleries – housed partly in Medeiros e Almeida's 19th-century mansion and partly in a modern wing. It includes paintings by Rubens, Pieter Bruegel II and Jacob Huysman, with a self-portrait by Rembrandt as one of the highlights. Other notable items include a tea set that belonged to Napoleon, some of the earliest Chinese porcelain to reach Europe and a collection of ornate watches and clocks.

7

Rossio

📍 N6 🚌 709, 711, 736 & many other routes Ⓜ Rossio

Formally called Praça Dom Pedro IV, this large square has been Lisbon's nerve centre for six centuries: the stage of bullfights, festivals, military parades and gruesome *autos da fé* (acts of faith). The sober Pombaline buildings are now occupied by shops and cafés. Centre stage is a statue of Dom Pedro IV, the first emperor of independent Brazil.

In the mid-19th century, the square was paved with wave-patterned mosaics that gave it the nickname of "Rolling Motion Square". The grey and white stone cubes were the first such designs to decorate the city's pavements.

On the north side of Rossio is the Teatro Nacional Dona Maria II, named after Dom Pedro's daughter. The Neo-Classical structure was built in the 1840s by the Italian architect Fortunato Lodi. The interior was destroyed by fire in 1964 and reconstructed in the 1970s. Atop the pediment is Gil Vicente (1465–1536), the founder of Portuguese theatre.

Café Nicola on the west side of the square was a favourite meeting place among writers, including the poet Manuel du Bocage (1765–1805), who was notorious for his satires.

Rossio's dramatic central fountain at sunset

↑ Cafés lining the grand Rua Augusta, framed by the triumphal arch

8

Rua Augusta

⑨N7 🚌711, 714, 732, 736, 759 & many other routes
Ⓜ Baixa-Chiado

A lively pedestrianized street decorated with mosaic pavements and lined with boutiques and cafés, Rua Augusta is the main tourist thoroughfare and the smartest in the Baixa. Street performers provide entertainment, while vendors sell souvenirs. The triumphal Arco da Rua Augusta, built to commemorate the city's recovery from the earthquake, was completed only in 1873. There are great views

from the top of the arch, which is accessed by an elevator.

The other main thoroughfares of the Baixa are Rua da Prata (silversmiths' street) and Rua do Ouro or Rua Áurea (goldsmiths' street). Cutting across these main streets are smaller streets that give glimpses up to the Bairro Alto to the west and Castelo de São Jorge (*p62*) to the east. Many streets retain shops that gave them their name: jewellers in Rua da Prata and Rua do Ouro and banks in Rua do Comércio.

In the heart of the Baixa is a small section of the Roman baths, located within the Banco Comercial Português in Rua dos Correeiros. The ruins and mosaics can be seen from the street window at the rear side of the bank; alternatively you can book ahead to visit the "museum" on 211 131 681.

9

Praça da Figueira

⑨N6 🚌714, 759, 760 & many other routes
🚊12, 15 Ⓜ Rossio

Before the 1755 earthquake, the square next to Rossio was the site of the Hospital de Todos-os-Santos (All Saints). In Pombal's new design for

→ Equestrian statue of João I standing in Praça da Figueira

EAT

Bonjardim, Rei dos Frangos
On a side street, this is the ideal place to sample Portugal's spit-roast chicken – with or without fiery piri-piri sauce.

⑨M6 🏠Travessa de Santo Antão 11-18
📞213 424 389
❌Wed in winter

 €€€

Cervejaria Ribadouro
Set in a striking 1920s building, this bustling restaurant and brewery does a strong line in fresh seafood.

⑨M5 🏠Avenida da Liberdade 155
🌐cervejariaribadouro.pt

€€€

Confeitaria Nacional
This historic café opened in 1829 and still serves a tempting array of pastries, teas and strong coffee.

⑨N6 🏠Praça da Figueira 18
📞213 424 470

 €€€

the Baixa, the square took on the role of the city's central marketplace. In 1885 a covered market was built, but this was pulled down in the 1950s. Today, the four-storey buildings are given over to hotels, shops and cafés and the square is no longer a marketplace. Perhaps its most eye-catching feature is the multitude of pigeons that perch on the pedestal supporting Leopoldo de Almeida's bronze equestrian statue of João I, erected in 1971.

Museu da Sociedade de Geografia

⑩ ⓂⓌ

📍M5 🏛Rua das Portas de Santo Antão 100 ☎213 425 401 🚌709, 711, 736 Ⓜ Restauradores ⏰11am-12:45pm, 2-4:45pm Mon-Fri

This museum houses an idiosyncratic ethnographical collection brought back from Portugal's former colonies. On display are circumcision masks from Guinea Bissau, musical instruments and snake spears. From Angola there are neck rests to sustain coiffures and the original *padrão* – the pillar erected by the Portuguese in 1482 to mark their sovereignty over the colony.

Núcleo Arqueológico

⑪ Ⓜ

📍N7 🏛Rua dos Correeiros 21 ☎211 131 004 ⏰10am-noon, 2-5pm Mon-Sat

Late-20th-century renovation works on this site uncovered archaeological finds, many dating back over 2,500 years. These have been preserved, often under glass flooring, and today can be visited in situ as part of a free and interesting guided tour. The cramped underground walkways provide a fascinating insight into Lisbon's history, from pre-Roman times to the 18th century. Displays range from the remains of Roman fish-preserving tanks to wooden pillars used to prop up Baixa's buildings when it was rebuilt on waterlogged land after the earthquake of 1755.

MUDE (Museu do Design e da Moda)

⑫

📍N7 🏛Rua Augusta 24 ⏰10am-6pm Tue-Sun (closed until 2019 for renovation, check website for updates) 🌐mude.pt

Anyone with an interest in design or fashion will want to linger at this tremendous collection of 20th-century classics from around the world, which traces the evolution of design from the 1930s onwards. The bulk of the pieces on display are from the private collection of Francisco Capelo, which the wealthy economist bequeathed to the state in 2003.

Exhibits are overhauled regularly, but usually feature the likes of "Marilyn's lips" (Bocca's iconic mouth-shaped sofa), furniture by Philippe Starck or Charles and Ray Eames, and wonderful haute couture from Vivienne Westwood, Jean-Paul Gaultier and Alexander McQueen.

Nossa Senhora da Conceição Velha

⑬

📍N7 🏛Rua da Alfândega ☎218 870 202 🚌759, 794 🚊18, 25 ⏰10am-2pm, 3-6pm daily

The elaborate Manueline doorway of the church is the only surviving feature from the original 16th-century Nossa Senhora da Misericórdia, which stood here until the 1755 earthquake. The portal is decorated with a profusion of Manueline detail, including angels, beasts, flowers and the cross of the Order of Christ. In the tympanum, the Virgin Mary spreads her protective mantle over various contemporary figures. These include Pope Leo X, Manuel I and his sister, Queen Leonor, widow of João II. It was Leonor who founded the original Misericórdia (alms house) on the site of a former synagogue.

🔍 HIDDEN GEM
Elevador da Lavra

Seek out the Elevador da Lavra, one of the city's lesser-known street lifts located at the end of Largo da Anunciada. Dating back to 1884, it climbs up to the pretty Jardim do Torel gardens.

MUDE, with the Arco da Rua Augusta in the background ↓

A SHORT WALK
RESTAURADORES

Distance 1.3 km (0.8 miles) **Nearest station**
Restauradores metro **Time** 20 minutes

This is the busiest part of Lisbon, especially the central squares of Rossio and Praça da Figueira. Totally rebuilt after the earthquake of 1755, the area was one of Europe's first examples of town planning. Stroll the wide streets to admire the large Neo-Classical buildings, before absorbing more of the atmosphere and surroundings from one of the bustling pavement cafés. Nearby Rua das Portas de Santo Antão, a pedestrianized street where restaurants display tanks of live lobsters, allows for a more leisurely pace.

The Elevador da Glória funicular goes up the hill towards the Bairro Alto, as far as the Miradouro de São Pedro de Alcântara (p103).

Built by Italian architect Francesco Fabri, the magnificent 18th-century Palácio Foz is now home to a tourist office.

START

PRAÇA DOS RESTAURADORES

FINISH

T. DE SANTO A

This large tree- and café-lined square was named after the soldiers who gave their lives during the War of Restoration.

Restauradores

```
0 metres        50    N
0 yards         50    ↑
```

The Neo-Manueline Rossio Station boasts an eye-catching façade featuring two Moorish-style horseshoe arches.

← The ornate façade of Rossio railway station

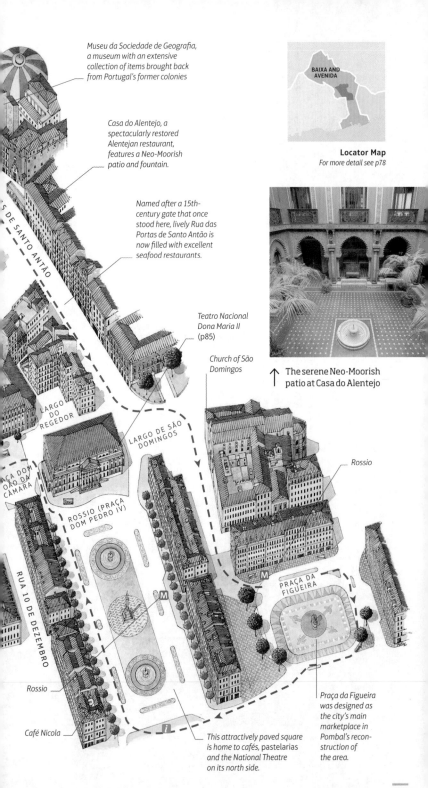

Museu da Sociedade de Geografia, a museum with an extensive collection of items brought back from Portugal's former colonies

Casa do Alentejo, a spectacularly restored Alentejan restaurant, features a Neo-Moorish patio and fountain.

Named after a 15th-century gate that once stood here, lively Rua das Portas de Santo Antão is now filled with excellent seafood restaurants.

Teatro Nacional Dona Maria II (p85)

Church of São Domingos

Locator Map
For more detail see p78

↑ The serene Neo-Moorish patio at Casa do Alentejo

DE SANTO ANTÃO

LARGO DO REGEDOR

LARGO DE SÃO DOMINGOS

ÇA DOM OÃO DA CÂMARA

ROSSIO (PRAÇA DOM PEDRO IV)

RUA 10 DE DEZEMBRO

Rossio

Rossio

Café Nicola

PRAÇA DA FIGUEIRA

This attractively paved square is home to cafés, pastelarias and the National Theatre on its north side.

Praça da Figueira was designed as the city's main marketplace in Pombal's recon- struction of the area.

BAIRRO ALTO AND ESTRELA

Laid out in a grid pattern in the late 16th century, the hilltop Bairro Alto was first settled by rich citizens who moved out of the disreputable Alfama. By the 19th century it had become a run-down area, attracting both prostitutes and the young bohemian set, and it soon developed into the city's main nightlife area. Small shops, family-run *tascas* (cheap restaurants) and bars moved in to form a district little changed today.

In contrast, the nearby elegant commercial district known as the Chiado is home to some of the city's oldest shops and cafés. Many of the area's original Belle Époque buildings were destroyed by a fire in 1988, but cleverly restored by architect Álvaro Siza Viera around the turn of the century. To the northwest, the Estrela quarter is centred on a huge domed basilica, built in 1790, while the smart district of Lapa, to the southwest, was laid out in the mid-18th century.

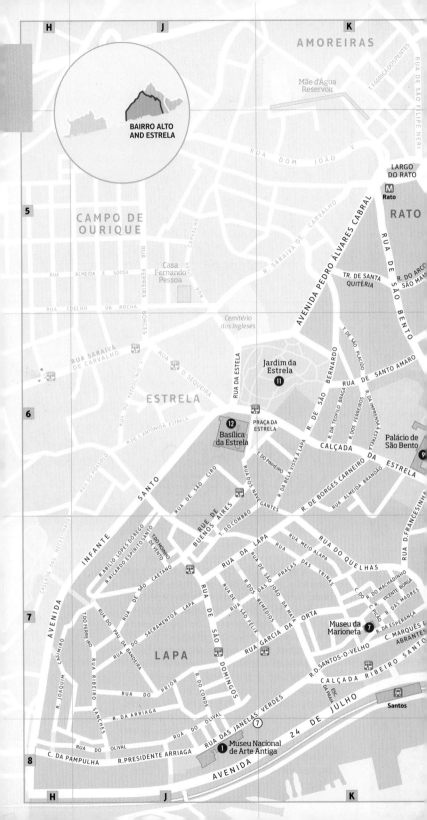

H   J   K

AMOREIRAS

Mãe d'Água
Reservoir

BAIRRO ALTO
AND ESTRELA

RUA DE SÃO FILIPE NERI
T. FÁBRICA DOS PENTES
RUA DE SÃO

RUA   DOM   JOÃO   V

LARGO
DO RATO
M Rato
RATO

5

CAMPO DE
OURIQUE

RUA   ALMEIDA   E   SOUSA

RUA FERREIRA BORGES

RUA ALMEIDA E SOUSA

Casa
Fernando
Pessoa

RUA   COELHO   DA   ROCHA

R. SARAIVA DE CARVALHO

AVENIDA PEDRO ÁLVARES CABRAL

TR. DE SANTA
QUITÉRIA

R. DO ARCO
SÃO MA

RUA DE SÃO BENTO

Cemitério
dos Ingleses

RUA SARAIVA
DE CARVALHO

RUA D. SEQUEIRA

RUA DO PATROCÍNIO À ESTRELA

RUA DA ESTELA

Jardim da
Estrela
11

R. DE SÃO BERNARDO

T. DE SÃO PLÁCIDO

R. DE TEÓFILO BRAGA

R. DOS FERREIROS

RUA DE SANTO AMARO

R. DA IMPRENSA À ESTRELA

6

ESTRELA

RUA D. DE ANTÓNIO À ESTRELA

12
Basílica
da Estrela

PRAÇA DA
ESTRELA

CALÇADA   DA   ESTRELA

Palácio de
São Bento
9

SANTO

RUA DE SÃO CIRO

T. DO PINHEIRO

RUA DOS NAVEGANTES

RUA DA BELA VISTA À LAPA

R. DE BORGES CARNEIRO

R. ALMEIDA BRANDÃO

RUA D. FRANCESINHA

INFANTE

RUA DE
BUENOS AIRES

T. DO COMBRO

RUA DA LAPA

RUA MEIO ALAPA

RUA DO QUELHAS

7

R. ABÍLIO LOPES DO REGO
R. RICARDO ESPÍRITO SANTO
T. DO MONINHO
T. DE BENTO

RUA DE SÃO CAETANO

RUA DE SÃO JOÃO DA MATA

PRAÇAS DAS
TRINAS

R. DOS REMÉDIOS

C. DO PICÃO
R. DO MACHADINHO
C. R. VICENTE BORGA
R. DAS MADRES
R. DA ESPERANÇA

Museu da
Marioneta
7

C. MARQUÊS F
ABRANTES

CALÇADA DAS NECESSIDADES

AVENIDA

T. DO FERREIRO

RUA DO PAU DA BANDEIRA

SACRAMENTO À LAPA

RUA DE SÃO DOMINGOS

RUA DE SÃO FÉLIX

RUA GARCIA DA ORTA

ESC. DA PRAIA

R. D. SANTOS-O-VELHO

CALÇADA   RIBEIRO   SANTOS

Santos

LAPA

R. JOAQUIM CASIMIRO

RUA RIBEIRO SANCHES

PRIOR

R. DO CONDE

RUA DAS JANELAS VERDES

R. DO OLIVAL

7

AVENIDA   24   DE   JULHO

8

C. DA PAMPULHA

R. PRESIDENTE ARRIAGA

RUA DO OLIVAL

1 Museu Nacional
de Arte Antiga

AVENIDA

H   J   K

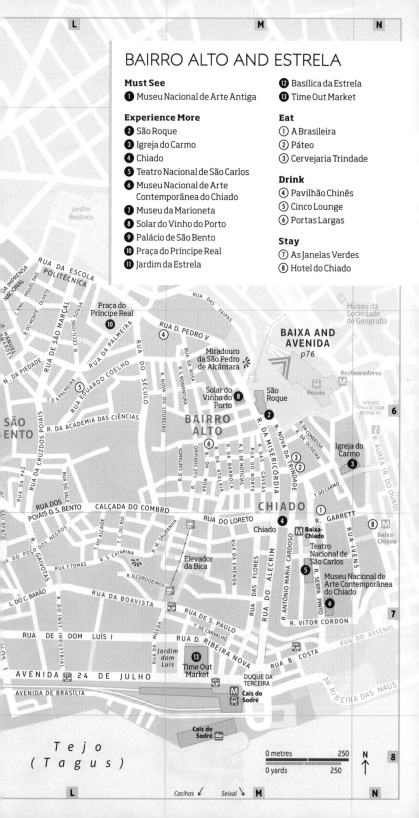

BAIRRO ALTO AND ESTRELA

Must See
1 Museu Nacional de Arte Antiga

Experience More
2 São Roque
3 Igreja do Carmo
4 Chiado
5 Teatro Nacional de São Carlos
6 Museu Nacional de Arte Contemporânea do Chiado
7 Museu da Marioneta
8 Solar do Vinho do Porto
9 Palácio de São Bento
10 Praça do Príncipe Real
11 Jardim da Estrela
12 Basílica da Estrela
13 Time Out Market

Eat
1 A Brasileira
2 Páteo
3 Cervejaria Trindade

Drink
4 Pavilhão Chinês
5 Cinco Lounge
6 Portas Largas

Stay
7 As Janelas Verdes
8 Hotel do Chiado

❶ 🖼️ 🍴 🖥️

MUSEU NACIONAL DE ARTE ANTIGA

📍 J8 🏛️ Rua das Janelas Verdes 🚌 613, 714, 727 🚊 15, 18 🕙 10am–6pm Tue–Sun 📅 1 Jan, Easter, 1 May, 25 Dec 🌐 museudearteantiga.pt

Portugal's national art collection is housed in a lemon-yellow 17th-century palace, originally built for the counts of Alvor. Among the exhibits are more state-designated "national treasures" than anywhere else in the country.

Inaugurated in 1884, the museum is known locally as the Museu das Janelas Verdes, a nod to the former green windows of the palace. In 1940, an annexe (including the main façade) was built on the site of the St Albert Carmelite monastery, which was partially demolished between 1910 and 1920. All that survived was a chapel, now integrated into the museum (although currently closed for restoration). After an afternoon's culture, the magnificent garden overlooking the Tagus offers an oasis of calm, plus an adjoining restaurant that serves delicious coffee and pastries. The museum's collection emphasizes Portuguese works, as well as paintings, artifacts and an extensive collection of jewellery from around the world. Highlights of the permanent collection include the exquisite 16th-century Namban screens, which depict contemporary Japanese trade with Portugal.

💬 INSIDER TIP
Into the Gardens

Once you've had your fill of culture amid the galleries, head for the sun-dappled gardens, where sculptures and sea views create a relaxing and pleasant place to unwind.

→
The museum's walls and pretty gardens, within which sits a café (inset)

1 The gallery of Portuguese painting and sculpture displays its exhibits in a sparse, dramatic arrangement.

2 This statue of St Leonard is by the renowned Florentine sculptor Andrea della Robbia (1435–1525).

3 Visitors admire *The Temptation of St Anthony*, a depiction of spiritual torment by the Dutch master of fantasy, Hieronymus Bosch (1450–1516).

40,000
—
The number of works of art housed in the museum.

The museum's bright, wide galleries lined with priceless paintings ↑

Exploring the Collections

The museum has the largest collection of paintings in Portugal, including an extensive treasury of early religious works by Portuguese artists. The majority of exhibits came from convents and monasteries following the suppression of religious orders in 1834. There are also wide-ranging displays of sculpture, silverware, porcelain and applied arts, giving an overview of Portuguese art from the Middle Ages to the 19th century, complemented by fine European and Eastern pieces. The theme of the Discoveries is ever-present, illustrating Portugal's links with Brazil, Africa, India, China and Japan.

Did You Know?

Hieronymus Bosch never dated his works, so we can't be exactly sure when they were painted.

Visitors admiring the *São Vicente de Fora* polyptych, one of the museum's most important pieces ↑

Must See

Top Collections

European Art

▶ Paintings by European artists, dating from the 14th to the 19th century, hang chronologically on the ground floor. Most of the works in this section were donated from private collections, contributing to the great diversity of works on display. Among the most notable works are *Salomé* by Lucus Cranach the Elder (1472-1553) and *The Temptation of St Anthony* by Hieronymus Bosch (1450-1516).

Portugese Painting and Sculpture

Many of the earliest works of art are by the Portuguese primitive painters, who were influenced by a Flemish trend of realistic detail. Thought to be by Nuno Gonçalves, the *São Vicente de Fora* polyptych, which shows religious, as well as contemporary figures, is an invaluable historical and social document. The sculpture collection includes many Gothic polychrome stone and wood statues.

Portuguese and Chinese Ceramics

The collection of Chinese porcelain and Portuguese faïence showcases the reciprocal influence between Far Eastern and Portuguese potters. From the 16th century, Portuguese ceramics show a marked influence of Ming, and conversely, Chinese pieces bear Portuguese motifs such as coats of arms. By the mid-18th century, an increasingly personalized, European style emerged among Portuguese potters, using popular, rustic designs.

Asian and African Art

The collection of ivories and furniture, with their European motifs, further illustrates the reciprocal influences of Portugal and her colonies. The 16th-century vogue for the exotic gave rise to a huge demand for items such as carved ivory hunting horns from Africa. The 16th- and 17th-century Japanese Namban screens show the Portuguese trading in Japan. *Namban-jin* (barbarians from the south) is the name the Japanese gave to the Portuguese.

Silver, Gold and Jewellery

◀ Among the ecclesiastical treasures are King Sancho I's 1214 gold cross and the 1506 Belém monstrance. The rich collection of jewels came from convents, originally donated by wealthy novices on entering religious orders.

Decorative Arts

Furniture, tapestries and textiles, liturgical vestments and bishops' mitres are among the wide range of objects on display. The furniture collection includes many pieces from Portuguese and other European royal courts. Among the textiles are 17th-century bedspreads, tapestries (many of Flemish origin, such as the 16th-century Baptism of Christ), embroidered rugs and Arraiolos carpets.

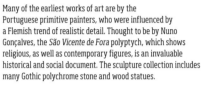

TOP 5 UNMISSABLE EXHIBITS

Ivory Salt Cellar
Portuguese dignitaries are carved in ivory on this 16th-century West African salt shaker.

The Chapel of St Albert
Admire the Baroque interior, covered in blue-and-white *azulejos*.

Faïence Violin
Portraits of Italian composers decorate this ceramic piece.

Salomé
Lucus Cranach the Elder's study of virtue or seductive perversion.

The Temptations of St Anthony
A fantastical oil-on-oak triptych.

EXPERIENCE MORE

2

São Roque

📍M6 🏛Largo Trindade
Coelho 📞213 235 444
🚌758 🕐Apr–Sep: 2–7pm
Mon, 9am–7pm Tue–Sun (to
8pm Thu); Oct–Mar: 2–6pm
Mon, 9am–6pm Tue–Sun
🚫Public hols

São Roque's plain façade belies
a rich interior. The church was
founded at the end of the 16th
century by the Jesuit Order,
then at the peak of its power.
In 1742, the Chapel of St John
the Baptist was commissioned
by the prodigal João V from
Italian architects Luigi Vanvitelli
and Nicola Salvi. Constructed
in Rome and embellished with
jewels, precious marbles, gold,
silver and mosaics, the chapel
was given the pope's blessing
in the church of Sant'Antonio
dei Portoghesi in Rome, dis-
mantled and sent to Lisbon
in three ships.

Among the church's many
tiles, the oldest and most
interesting are those in the
third chapel on the right,
dating from the 16th century
and dedicated to São Roque
(St Roch), protector against

the plague. Other features
of the church are the scenes
of the Apocalypse painted
on the ceiling.

3

Igreja do Carmo

📍M6 🏛Largo do Carmo
📞213 460 473 🚌758 🚋28
Ⓜ Baixa-Chiado 🕐10am–
6pm Mon–Sat (to 7pm Jun–
Sep) 🚫1 Jan, 1 May, 25 Dec

The Gothic ruins of this
Carmelite church, built on a
slope overlooking the Baixa,
are evocative reminders of the
devastation left by the earthquake of 1755. The church
collapsed during Mass, depo-
siting tons of masonry on to
the people below. Founded
in the late 14th century by
Nuno Álvares Pereira, the

↓ Interior of São Roque,
the earliest Jesuit
church in Lisbon

Did You Know?

Fernando Pessoa liked
to write under distinct
literary personas,
which he called
"heteronyms".

commander who became a
member of the Carmelite
Order, the church was at one
time the biggest in Lisbon.
Today, the main body of the
church and the chancel, whose
roof withstood the earthquake,
houses the Museu do Carmo,
with a small, heterogeneous
collection of sarcophagi,
statuary, ceramics and mosaics.

Among more ancient finds
from Europe are a remnant of
a Visigothic pillar and a Roman
tomb carved with reliefs
depicting the Muses. There are
also finds from Mexico and
South America, including
ancient mummies.

DRINK

Pavilhão Chinês
This quirky bar is packed with a bizarre array of collector's items, from dolls to model planes, and also features a strong cocktail list.

📍L6 ⌂Rua Dom Pedro V 89
☎213 424 729

Cinco Lounge
Credited with making cocktails cool in Lisbon, this smart and very chic bar offers over 100 options, ranging from classics to the more experimental.

📍L6 ⌂Rua Ruben A. Leitão 17a
🌐cincolounge.com

Portas Largas
A buzzy, traditional tavern with live music and well-priced drinks, where the revelry spills out onto the street.

📍M6 ⌂Rua da Atalaia 103-105
☎218 466 379

Chiado

📍M7 🚌758 🚋28
Ⓜ Baixa-Chiado

Statues of literary figures can be found in this area, known for its intellectual associations. A bronze statue by sculptor Lagoa Henriques

THE CHIADO FIRE
On 25 August 1988, a disastrous fire began in a store in Rua do Carmo, the street that links the Baixa with the Bairro Alto. Fire engines were unable to enter this pedestrianized street and the fire spread into Rua Garrett. Important 18th-century buildings were destroyed. The renovation project, headed by Portuguese architect Álvaro Siza Vieira, preserved many original façades.

↑ Statue of poet Fernando Pessoa outside the café A Brasileira

depicts Fernando Pessoa, Portugal's great Modernist poet, sitting at a table outside the café A Brasileira, once a favourite rendezvous of the city's intellectuals.

Rua Garrett, named after the author and poet João Almeida Garrett (1799–1854), descending from Largo do Chiado towards the Baixa, is known for its cafés and shops. Devastated by fire in 1988, the former elegance of this quarter has now been restored.

Teatro Nacional de São Carlos

📍M7 ⌂Rua Serpa Pinto 9
🚌758, 790 🚋28 Ⓜ Baixa-Chiado 🌐tnsc.pt

Replacing a former opera house that was ruined by the earthquake of 1755, the Teatro de São Carlos was built in 1792–5 by José da Costa e Silva. Inspired by the design of great Italian theatres such as La Scala in Milan, the building has a beautifully proportioned façade and an enchanting Rococo interior. Views of the exterior, however, are spoiled by the car park, invariably crammed, which occupies the square in front.

The opera season lasts from September to June, but concerts and ballets are also staged here at other times of the year. The opera house is also home to the Portuguese Symphonic Orchestra.

↑ Paintings and sculpture at Museu Nacional de Arte Contemporânea do Chiado

6

Museu Nacional de Arte Contemporânea do Chiado

📍 M7 🏛 Rua Serpa Pinto 4-6 🚌 758, 790 🚃 28 Ⓜ Baixa-Chiado 🕐 10am-6pm Tue-Sun 🚫 1 Jan, Easter, 1 May, 25 Dec 🌐 museuartecontemporanea.gov.pt

The National Museum of Contemporary Art moved to this stylishly restored warehouse in 1994. The paintings and sculpture are arranged over three floors in seven rooms. Each room has a different theme illustrating the development from Romanticism to Modernism. The majority are Portuguese works, often showing a marked influence from other European countries – this is particularly noticeable in the 19th-century landscape painters who had contact with artists from the French Barbizon School. The few international works of art on display are mainly French sculpture from the late 19th century, including one by Rodin (1840–1917). There are also temporary exhibitions, which are held for "very new artists, preferably inspired by the permanent collection".

7

Museu da Marioneta

📍 K7 🏛 Convento das Bernardas, Rua da Esperança 146 🚌 713, 727, 760 🚃 15, 25 Ⓜ Cais do Sodré 🚆 Santos 🕐 10am-6pm Tue-Sun 🚫 1 Jan, 1 May, 24 & 25 Dec 🌐 museudamarioneta.pt

This small puppet museum, housed in an elegantly refurbished convent building, includes characters from 17th- and 18th-century theatre and opera, including jesters, devils, knights and satirical figures. Many of the puppets possess gruesome, contorted features that are unlikely to appeal to small children. The museum explains the history of the art form and runs videos of puppet shows. Check the website

↑ Puppets from the collection at Museu da Marioneta

to see if a live performance is being held on the small stage. There is also a space for children's entertainment and learning.

Miradouro da São Pedro de Alcântara

This *miradouro* boasts a sweeping vista of eastern Lisbon. A tiled map, placed against the balustrade, helps you locate the landmarks. The view is most attractive at sunset and by night, when the castle is floodlit and the terrace becomes a meeting point for young Lisboetas.

8

Solar do Vinho do Porto

Q M6 **A** Rua de São Pedro de Alcântara 45 **C** 213 475 707 **E** 758 **F** 28 **O** Elevador da Glória: 11am-midnight Mon-Fri, 3pm-midnight Sat (times may vary, call ahead) **Q** Public hols

The Portuguese word *solar* means mansion or manor house, and the Solar do Vinho do Porto occupies the ground floor of an 18th-century mansion. The building was once owned by the German architect Johann Friedrich Ludwig (Ludovice), who built the monastery at Mafra (*p160*). The port wine institute of Porto runs a pleasant bar here for the promotion of port. Nearly 200 types of port are listed in the lengthy drinks menu, with every producer represented and including some rarities. Unfortunately, many of the listed wines are often unavailable. All but the vintage ports are sold by the glass, with prices ranging from €1.50 for the simplest ruby to €13.30 for a glass of 40-year-old tawny.

9

Palácio de São Bento

Q K6 **A** Largo das Cortes **C** 213 919 620 **E** 790 **F** 28 **O** By appt last Sat of month, 3pm & 4pm; **W** parlamento.pt

Also known as the Assembleia da República, this massive white Neo-Classical building started life in the late 1500s as the Benedictine monastery of São Bento. After the dissolution of the religious orders in 1834, the building became the seat of parliament, known as the Palácio das Cortes. The interior is grand with marble pillars and Neo-Classical statues.

10

Praça do Príncipe Real

Q L6 **E** 758

Originally laid out in 1860 as a prime residential neighbour-hood, Praça do Príncipe Real still retains its charming air of affluence. Smartly painted mansions surround a park with a café, statuary and some splendid robinia, magnolia and Judas trees. The branches of a huge cedar tree have been trained on a trellis, creating a wide shady spot for the locals who play cards beneath it. On the large square, at No 26, the eye-catching white Neo-Moorish building with domes houses a shopping gallery.

> Originally laid out in 1860 as a prime residential neighbourhood, Praça do Príncipe Real still retains its charming air of affluence.

↑ Tree-shaded park at the heart of Praça do Príncipe Real

The sun-dappled streets of the Chiado district

↑ The wrought-iron bandstand at the centre of Jardim da Estrela

⓫ 🖵 Jardim da Estrela

📍 K6 🏠 Praça da Estrela
🚎 720, 738 🚋 25, 28 Ⓜ Rato
🕐 7am–midnight daily

Laid out in the middle of the 19th century, opposite the Basílica da Estrela, the popular gardens are a focal part of the Estrela quarter. Picturesque and serene, they provide an oasis from the hustle and bustle of the city.

Local families congregate here at weekends to feed the carp and ducks in the lake, sit at the waterside café or wander among the flower beds, plants and trees. The formal gardens are planted with herbaceous borders and shrubs surrounding plane trees and elms. The central feature of the park is a green wrought-iron bandstand, decorated with elegant filigree, where musicians strike up in the summer

CONTEMPORARY PORTUGUESE CUISINE

Exploding olives and acorn ice cream are some of the unusual offerings now found at Lisbon's innovative new restaurants. Spear-headed by the likes of José Avillez *(right)*, creator of Belcanto, the first Lisbon restaurant to earn two Michelin stars, contemporary Portuguese dining focuses on finding unexpected, top-quality local ingredients to lift traditional recipes into something unforgettable.

months. The bandstand was built in 1884 and originally stood on the Passeio Público, before the creation of Avenida da Liberdade *(p84)*.

The English Cemetery to the north of the gardens is best known as the burial place of Henry Fielding (1707–54), the English novelist and playwright who died in Lisbon at the age of 47. The *Journal of a Voyage to Lisbon*, published post-humously in 1775, recounts his last voyage to Portugal, made in a fruitless attempt to recover his failing health.

⓬ Basílica da Estrela

📍 J6 🏠 Praça da Estrela
📞 213 960 915 🚎 720, 738
🚋 25, 28 🕐 9am–1pm, 3–7:30pm Mon–Fri (to 8pm Sat & Sun); large groups by appointment

In the second half of the 18th century Maria I *(p159)*, daughter of José I, vowed she would build a church if she bore a son and heir to the throne. Her wish was granted and construction of the basilica began in 1779. Her son José, however, died of smallpox two years before the comple-tion of the church in 1790.

The huge domed Basílica da Estrela, which is proudly set on a hill overlooking the west of the city, is one of Lisbon's most remarkable landmarks. A simpler version of the basilica at Mafra *(p160)*, this church was built by architects from the Mafra School in late-Baroque and Neo-Classical style. The façade is flanked by twin bell towers and decorated with an array of statues of saints and allegorical figures.

The spacious, awe-inspiring interior, where light streams down from the pierced dome, is clad in grey, pink and yellow marble. The elaborate Empire-style tomb of Queen Maria I, who died in Brazil, lies in the right transept. Locked in a room nearby is Machado de

The huge domed Basílica da Estrela, which is proudly set on a hill overlooking the west of the city, is one of Lisbon's most remarkable landmarks.

Castro's extraordinary nativity scene, composed of over 500 cork-and-terracotta figures. To see it, ask the sacristan.

Be sure to climb the dome's steep stone steps to access the flat roof above the Basílica, where you'll find breathtaking views of the western city – and down into the church below.

---

13 Ⓨ Ⓓ Ⓐ

Time Out Market (Mercado da Ribeira)

📍 M7 🏠 Avenida 24 de Julho ⏰ 10am-midnight Sun-Wed, 10am-2am Thu-Sat; fish, fruit and vegetable market: 6am-2pm Mon-Sat 🌐 timeout market.com

Lisbon's historic Mercado da Ribeira opened for business in 1930, and has served as the city's main fruit and vegetable market ever since. It was rejuvenated in 2014, by incorporating the many food and drink stalls of the world's first Time Out Market, which now occupy most of the cavernous central hall.

Stake your claim on one of the communal benches and sample the diverse array of produce on offer from some of Lisbon's best-known food outlets (including Henrique Sá Pessoa from Michelin-starred restaurant Alma). You can enjoy anything from burgers and sushi to fine cheeses, *pastéis de nata* and ice cream, while champagne bars and wine, beer or juice stalls cater to the thirsty.

There are further bars and restaurants around the outside of the market and on the first floor, which has a music venue for concerts. The concept has proved overwhelmingly successful – attracting over three million visitors a year – and Time Out has subsequently opened similar markets in the US.

↓ The Time Out Market's cavernous food court, thronging with visitors

EAT

A Brasileira
The intellectuals who made this 1905 café famous are gone, but its Art Deco interior and bar filled with tempting pastries remain a draw.

📍 M6 🏠 Rua Garrett 120 📞 213 469 541

€ⓔⓔ

Páteo
Occupying a covered patio inside a former monastery, this lovely space specializes in quality fish and seafood, prepared by chef José Avillez.

📍 M6 🏠 Bairro do Avillez, 18 Rua Nova da Trindade 18 📞 215 830 290

€ⓔⓔ

Cervejaria Trindade
Famed for its beautiful *azulejos*, this 1830s beer hall serves tasty seafood and steak.

📍 M6 🏠 Rua Nova da Trindade 20 📞 213 423 506

€ⓔⓔ

A SHORT WALK

BAIRRO ALTO AND CHIADO

Distance 1 km (0.6 miles) **Nearest station**
Baixa-Chiado metro **Time** 15 minutes

The Bairro Alto (high quarter) is a fascinating plot of
cobbled streets adjacent to the Carmo and Chiado
areas. Since the 1980s, this has been Lisbon's best-
known nightlife zone, with countless small bars and
restaurants alongside the older *casas de fado*.
While more modern buildings have also
sprung up in recent years, the quarter remains
a lively, authentic part of the city to wander.
In contrast, the Chiado presents a more
manicured façade, filled as it is with elegant
shops and old-style cafés that extend down
from Praça Luís de Camões towards Rua do
Carmo and the Baixa. Major renovation
work has taken place here since a fire
in 1988 *(p101)* destroyed many of
the original buildings.

RUA DO NORTE

RUA DAS GÁVEAS

Praça Luís de Camões

*Tavares, at No 37 Rua da
Misericórdia, first opened as a
café in 1784 and is today an
elegant restaurant with fine
early-20th-century interiors.*

RUA DO ALECRIM

L. DO CHIADO

RUA GARRETT

*This statue of realist novelist
Eça de Queirós (1845–1900),
by Teixeira Lopes, was
erected in 1903.*

*Largo do Chiado,
flanked by the
churches of Loreto
and Nossa Senhora
da Encarnação*

Ⓜ

Baixa-Chiado

*A Brasileira,
a historic café on
Largo do Chiado adorned
with gilded mirrors*

*Rua Garrett,
the Chiado's main
shopping street*

← Diners seated along the
patterned walls of the
Cervejaria Trindade

The Museu de São Roque
houses an interesting
exhibition of religious
artifacts and explains
the history of the church
next door.

FINISH

Opulent mosaics and
semiprecious stones adorn
the Baroque Capela de São
João inside the 16th-century
church of São Roque.

Cervejaria Trindade, a
popular beer hall and
restaurant decorated
with azulejo panels

Teatro da Trindade

Largo Rafael
Bordalo Pinheiro,
where the tiled
façade of a house
dating from 1864
features elaborate
allegorical figures

RUA DA MISERICÓRDIA

RUA NOVA DA TRINDADE

RUA DA TRINDADE

TRAVESSA DO CARMO

LARGO DO CARMO

C. DO SACRAMENTO

START

↑ The delicate pillars
and arcades of the
Igreja do Carmo

Igreja do Carmo, a Carmelite
church whose graceful skeletal
arches stand as a reminder of the
earthquake of 1755. The chancel and
main body of the church house an
archaeological museum.

Elevador de Santa Justa (p82),
an ornate street lift offering
direct access from the Baixa
to the Bairro Alto district

Shops in Rua do Carmo,
restored and renewed
after the devastating
Chiado fire

| 0 metres | | 50 |
| 0 yards | | 50 |

N

A LONG WALK
BAIRRO ALTO AND ESTRELA

Distance: 2.5 km (1.5 miles) **Walking time:** 50 minutes **Nearest Station:** Praça da Estrela tram stop **Difficulty:** Steep in places, with steps

The mainly residential Estrela neighbourhood is typical of well-to-do west Lisbon. The Portuguese parliament lies to the east, then the terrain rises to Praça do Príncipe Real. This sloping neighbourhood with its small, bustling streets and energetic nightlife is typically Lisboetan. On the other side of the ridge, the Jardim Botânico descends steeply towards the city centre.

Locator Map
For more detail see p78 and p94

BAIXA AND AVENIDA

BAIRRO ALTO AND ESTRELA

Antique shops and buildings with attractively tiled façades line Rua de São Bento.

*Enjoy a stroll through the pleasant **Jardim da Estrela** (p106). Admire the park's numerous statues, exotic planting and ornate wrought-iron bandstand.*

Cemitério dos Ingleses

RATO

Rato

Jardim da Estrela

ESTRELA

START

Basílica da Estrela

PRAÇA DA ESTRELA

CALÇADA DA ESTRELA

Palácio de São Bento

*Begin the walk at **Basílica da Estrela** (p106). With its huge imposing dome, this historic church is one of Lisbon's great landmarks.*

*The grand, Neo-Classical **Palácio de São Bento** (p103) is the seat of the Assembly of the Republic, the Portuguese parliament.*

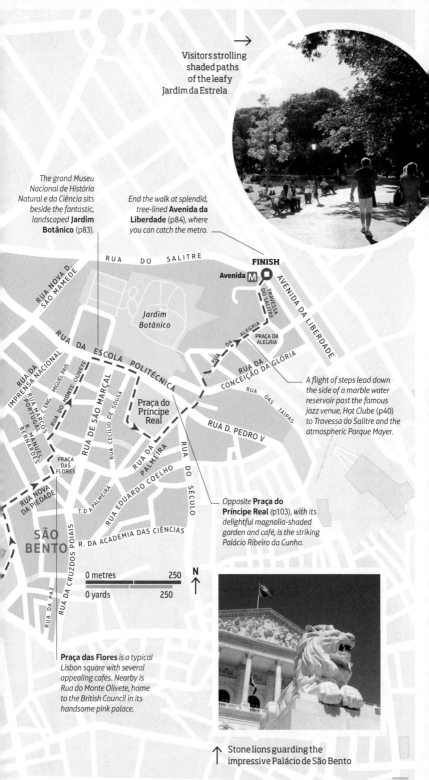

→ Visitors strolling shaded paths of the leafy Jardim da Estrela

The grand Museu Nacional de História Natural e da Ciência sits beside the fantastic, landscaped **Jardim Botânico** (p83).

End the walk at splendid, tree-lined **Avenida da Liberdade** (p84), *where you can catch the metro.*

FINISH

Avenida Ⓜ

AVENIDA DA LIBERDADE

TRAVESSA DO SALITRE

RUA DO SALITRE

RUA NOVA D. SÃO MAMEDE

Jardim Botânico

RUA DA ESCOLA POLITÉCNICA

RUA DA ALEGRIA

PRAÇA DA ALEGRIA

RUA DA CONCEIÇÃO DA GLÓRIA

RUA DAS TAIPAS

A flight of steps lead down the side of a marble water reservoir past the famous jazz venue, Hot Clube (p40) to Travessa do Salitre and the atmospheric Parque Mayer.

RUA DA IMPRENSA NACIONAL

RUA C. ENG. MIGUEL PAIS

RUA DO MONTE OLIVETE

RUA DE SÃO MARÇAL

RUA CECÍLIO DE SOUSA

RUA MARCOS PORTUGAL

RUA MANUEL BERNARDES

Praça do Príncipe Real

RUA D. PEDRO V

RUA DA PALMEIRA

RUA DO SÉCULO

PRAÇA DAS FLORES

T. D A PALMEIRA

RUA EDUARDO COELHO

RUA NOVA DA PIEDADE

SÃO BENTO

R. DA ACADEMIA DAS CIÊNCIAS

RUA DA CRUZADOS POIAIS

RUA DA PAZ

Opposite **Praça do Príncipe Real** (p103), *with its delightful magnolia-shaded garden and café, is the striking Palácio Ribeiro da Cunha.*

| 0 metres | 250 |
| 0 yards | 250 |

N ↑

Praça das Flores *is a typical Lisbon square with several appealing cafés. Nearby is Rua do Monte Olivete, home to the British Council in its handsome pink palace.*

↑ Stone lions guarding the impressive Palácio de São Bento

BELÉM

Perched as it is at the mouth of the Tagus river, where the caravels launched their voyages, Belém is inextricably linked with Portugal's golden Age of Discovery. When Manuel I came to power in 1495 he reaped the profits of those heady days of expansion, using it to build grandiose monuments and churches that mirrored the spirit of the time. Two of the finest examples of this exuberant and exotic Manueline style of architecture are the Mosteiro dos Jerónimos and the Torre de Belém.

Following the earthquake of 1775, José I installed his court in a series of tents in Belém's hills, the site of the Palácio Nacional da Ajuda, where it would remain for nearly three decades. This move attracted commerce to the area and Belém continued to thrive. The 19th-century main street has largely resisted modernization, and the Antiga Confeiteria de Belém, celebrated as the birthplace of Lisbon's iconic custard tart, can still be visited at its original site.

BELÉM

Must Sees
1 Mosteiro dos Jerónimos
2 Torre de Belém

Experience More
3 Museu Nacional dos Coches
4 Palácio de Belém
5 Jardim Botânico Tropical
6 Museu Nacional de Arqueologia
7 Planetário Calouste Gulbenkian
8 Museu de Marinha
9 Centro Cultural de Belém
10 Padrão dos Descobrimentos
11 Museu Colecção Berardo

12 MAAT – Museu de Arte, Arquitetura e Tecnologia
13 Ermida de São Jerónimo
14 Igreja da Memória
15 Jardim Botânico da Ajuda
16 Palácio Nacional da Ajuda

Stay
1 Jerónimos 8
2 Altis Belém
3 Pestana Palace

Eat
4 Antiga Confeitaria de Belém

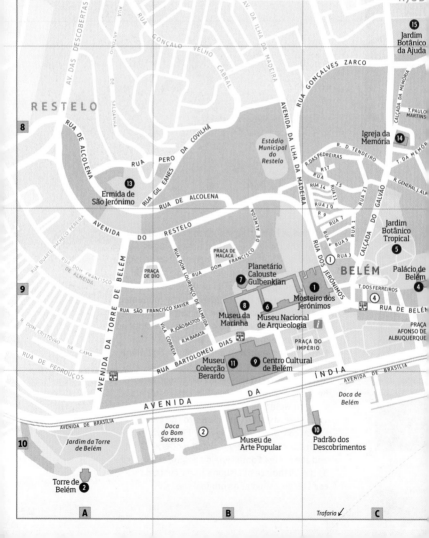

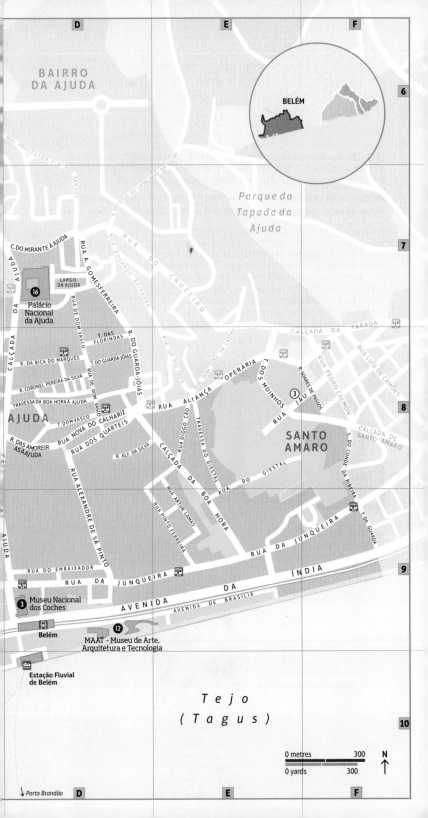

MOSTEIRO DOS JERÓNIMOS

⊙ C9 **⌂ Praça do Império (combined ticket for monastery and Torre de Belém available)** 🚌 714, 727, 728, 729, 751 🚋 15 🚆 Belém 🕐 10am-5:30pm Tue-Sun (to 6:30pm May-Sep) ⊘ Public hols 🌐 mosteirojeronimos.gov.pt

Belém's most popular tourist attraction, this highly ornate monastery is a National Monument and was designated a UNESCO World Heritage Site in 1983.

A monument to the wealth of the Age of Discovery (p53), the monastery was commissioned by Manuel I around 1501, and was financed largely by "pepper money" – a tax levied on spices, precious stones and gold. The monastery was cared for by the Order of St Jerome (Hieronymites) until 1834, when all religious orders were disbanded. Great figures from Portugal's history are entombed here – but one tomb stands empty: that of the "longed for" Dom Sebastião, the young king who never returned from battle in 1578.

The walls of the refectory are tiled with 18th-century azulejos.

↑ The monastery's exterior, designed to emphasize the Portuguese empire's wealth

→ The decorated exterior and interior of the Mosteiro dos Jerónimos

The modern wing, built in 1850 in Neo-Manueline style, houses the Museu Nacional de Arqueologia (p121).

The west portal, designed by the French sculptor Nicolau Chanterène

① Slender pillars rise like palm trees to the spectacular vaulted roof in the church of Santa Maria.

② The 19th-century tomb of navigator Vasco da Gama is festooned with seafaring symbols.

③ João de Castilho's pure Manueline cloisters are adorned with delicate tracery and richly carved arches.

The chapterhouse holds the tomb of Alexandre Herculano, historian and first mayor of Belém.

Cloister

Did You Know?

Eighteenth-century *azulejos* in the rectory depict the Feeding of the Five Thousand.

The chancel, commissioned in 1572 by Dona Catarina, the wife of João III

The empty tomb of the "longed for" Dom Sebastião

The geometrical lines of the south portal are covered with exuberant decoration.

2 ⚒

TORRE DE BELÉM

📍 A10 🚌 Avenida de Brasilia 🚌 727, 728, 729, 751 🚋 15
🚇 Belém 🕐 10am–6:30pm Tue–Sun (to 5:30pm Apr–Oct)
🗓 1 Jan, Easter Sun, 1 May, 13 Jun, 25 Dec 🌐 torrebelem.gov.pt

Set like a giant stone rook at the edge of the Tagus, this elaborate tower showcases some of Belém's best Manueline architecture. After admiring the intricate exterior, climb its narrow spiral staircase for breathtaking views.

Commissioned by Manuel I, the tower was built as a fortress in 1514–20, and soon became a symbol of Portugal's great era of expansion. The real beauty of this Manueline gem lies in the decoration of the exterior. Adorned with rope carved in stone, it has openwork balconies, Moorish-style watchtowers and distinctive battlements in the shape of shields. The Gothic interior below the terrace, which served as a storeroom for arms and a prison, is very austere, but the private quarters in the tower are worth visiting for the loggia and the panorama.

→

The stone fortress, a symbol of Portugal's seafaring power

Did You Know?

The tower's real name is the Torre de São Vicente, after the city's patron saint.

Battlements, decorated with the cross of the Order of Christ

The Italian-inspired arcaded loggia is a light touch along the battlements.

Sentry posts

Statue of the Virgin Mary, a symbol of protection for sailors

The vaulted dungeon was used as a prison until the 19th century.

↑ The Torre de Belém, sitting at the edge of the Tagus river

↑ Open cloister in the tower, designed to dispel cannon smoke

— King's room

— Entrance

Gangway to shore

EXPERIENCE MORE

3 🗲 Ⓜ 🖥 🛍

Museu Nacional dos Coches

📍D9 🏛 Avenida da Índia 136 🚌 714, 727, 728, 729, 751 🚊15 🚆 Belém 🕙10am–6pm Tue–Sun 🚫1 Jan, Easter, 1 May, 13 Jun, 24 & 25 Dec 🔗 museudoscoches.pt

This unique collection of coaches is arguably the finest in Europe. First established in the old Royal Riding School, the museum showcases a unique and opulent collection of coaches, carriages and sedan chairs dating from the 17th, 18th and 19th centuries. The collection was moved to a new, modern building by the Brazilian architect Paulo Mendes da Rocha, winner of the 2006 Pritzker Prize, in 2015.

The extra space enabled more modern vehicles to be added to the display. However, for most visitors the historic royal carriages still steal the show. Made in Portugal, Italy, France, Austria and Spain, carriages range from the plain to the preposterous. One of the earliest is the comparatively simple 17th-century leather and wood coach of Philip II

of Spain. As time goes by, the coaches become more sumptuous, the interiors lined with red velvet and gold, the exteriors carved and decorated with allegories and royal coats of arms. Three huge Baroque coaches made in Rome for the Portuguese ambassador to the Vatican, Dom Rodrigo Almeida e Menezes, Marquês de Abrantes, are the epitome of pomp, embellished with life-size gilded statues.

Further examples of royal carriages include two-wheeled cabriolets, landaus and pony-drawn chaises used by young members of the royal family. The 18th-century Eyeglass Chaise, whose black leather hood is pierced by sinister eye-like windows, was made during the Pombal era (p138), when lavish decoration was discouraged. The museology, installed in 2017, presents interactive displays that give context to the collection.

Made in Portugal, Italy, France, Austria and Spain, carriages range from the plain to the preposterous.

↑ Opulent carriages exibited at the Museu Nacional dos Coches

Did You Know?

Most of Belém's museums and historic buildings were built for the 1940 Lisbon Expo.

4

Palácio de Belém

📍C9 🏠Praça Afonso de Albuquerque 🚌714, 727, 728, 729, 751 🚋15 🚉Belém ⏰10:30am–4:30pm Sat; Museu da Presidência da República: 10am–6pm Tue-Sun 🚫Easter, 1 May, 25 Dec 🌐museu.presidencia.pt

Built by the Conde de Aveiras in 1559, before the Tagus had receded, this palace once had gardens bordering the river. In the 1700s it was bought by João V, who made it suitably lavish for his amorous liaisons.

When the 1755 earthquake struck, the king, José I, and his family were staying here and thus survived the devastation of central Lisbon. Fearing another tremor, the royal family temporarily set up camp in tents in the palace grounds, while the interior was used as a hospital. Today the elegant pink building is the official residence of the President of Portugal.

The Museu da Presidência da República holds personal items and state gifts of former presidents, as well as the official portrait gallery.

5

Jardim Botânico Tropical

📍C9 🏠Largo do Jerónimos 📞213 921 851 🚌714, 727, 728, 729, 751 🚋15 🚉Belém ⏰9am–8pm daily (to 5pm Oct-Mar) 🚫1 Jan, Easter, 25 Dec

Also known as the Jardim do Ultramar, this peaceful park with ponds, waterfowl and peacocks attracts surprisingly few visitors. Designed at the beginning of the 20th century as the research centre of the Institute for Tropical Sciences, it is more of an arboretum than a flower garden. The emphasis is on rare and endangered tropical and subtropical trees and plants. Among the most striking are dragon trees, native to the Canary Islands and Madeira, monkey puzzle trees from

STAY

Jerónimos 8
This sleek, modern hotel is at odds with its location in historic Belém close to the monastery.

📍C9 🏠Rua dos Jerónimos 8 🌐jeronimos8.com

€€€

Altis Belém
Beside the Tagus river, this ultra-modern hotel has a Michelin-starred restaurant and rooftop pool with city views.

📍B10 🏠Doca do Bom Sucesso 🌐altishotels.com.

€€€

Pestana Palace
The sumptuous interiors of this ornate palace are matched by lovely gardens with a pool and Chinese pavilion.

📍E8 🏠Rua Jau 54 🌐pestanapalace lisbon.com

€€€

Manicured gardens of the Palácio de Belém ↓

South America and a splendid avenue of Washington palms. The charming Oriental garden with its streams, bridges and hibiscus is heralded by a large Chinese-style gateway that represented Macau in the Exhibition of the Portuguese World in 1940.

The research buildings are located in the neighbouring Palácio dos Condes da Calheta, whose interior walls are covered with *azulejos* that span three centuries. Temporary exhibitions are held in the palace (closed 12:30–2pm).

6

Museu Nacional de Arqueologia

📍 B9 🏛 Praça do Império
🚌 714, 727, 728, 729, 751
🚊 15 🚋 Belém 🕐 10am–6pm Tue-Sun 🚫 1 Jan, Easter, 1 May, 13 Jun, 24 & 25 Dec 🌐 museunacionalarqueologia.gov.pt

The long west wing of the Mosteiro dos Jerónimos *(p116)*, which was formerly the monks' dormitory, has been an archaeological museum since 1893. Reconstructed in the middle of the 19th century, the building is a poor imitation of the Manueline

original. The museum houses Portugal's main archaeological research centre and the exhibits, from sites all over the country, include a gold Iron Age bracelet, Visigothic jewellery found in the Alentejo in southern Portugal, Roman ornaments, some fine Roman mosaics and early-8th-century Moorish artifacts.

The main Greco-Roman and Egyptian section is particularly strong on funerary art, featuring figurines, tombstones, masks, terracotta amulets and funeral cones inscribed with hieroglyphics alluding to the solar system, dating from 6000 BC.

The dimly lit Room of Treasures is full of exquisit gold and silver artifacts, including coins, necklaces, bracelets and other jewellery dating from 1800 to 500 BC. This room has been refurbished to allow more of the magnificent jewellery, unseen by the public for decades, to be displayed. In addition, the museum holds temporary exhibitions from time to time.

↑ An exhibition of pottery at the Museu Nacional de Arqueologia

7

Planetário Calouste Gulbenkian

📍 B9 🏛 Praça do Império
🚌 714, 727, 728, 751 🚊 15
🚋 Belém 🕐 Times vary, check website for details
🌐 ccm.marinha.pt

Financed by the Gulbenkian Foundation *(p132)* and built in 1965, this modern building sits incongruously beside the Jerónimos monastery. Inside, the planetarium reveals the mysteries of the cosmos. There are shows in Portuguese, English, Spanish and French several times a week, explaining the movement of the stars and our solar system, as well as presentations on the constellations or the Star of Bethlehem (Belém). The Hubble Vision show includes stunning images provided by the orbital telescope.

> **The long west wing of the Mosteiro dos Jerónimos, which was formerly the monks' dormitory, has been an archaeological museum since 1893.**

Museu de Marinha

📍 B9 🏛 Praça do Império
🚌 714, 727, 728, 729, 751
🚊 15 🚆 Belém ⏰ 10am–
6pm daily (to 5pm Oct–Apr)
🚫 1 Jan, Easter, 1 May,
25 Dec 🌐 ccm.marinha.pt

The Maritime Museum was inaugurated in 1962 in the west wing of the Jerónimos monastery (p116). It was here, in the chapel built by Henry the Navigator (p53), that mariners took Mass before embarking on their voyages. A hall devoted to the Discoveries illustrates the progress in shipbuilding from the mid-15th century, capitalizing on the experience of long-distance explorers. Small replicas show the transition from the barque to the lateen-rigged caravel, through the faster square-rigged caravel, to the Portuguese nau.

Also here are navigational instruments, astrolabes and replicas of 16th-century maps showing the world as it was known then. The stone pillars, carved with the Cross of the Knights of Christ, are replicas of the types of padrão set up as monuments to Portuguese sovereignty on the lands discovered.

Fine models of old sailing ships on display at the Museu de Marinha →

A series of rooms displaying models of modern Portuguese ships leads on to the Royal Quarters, where you can see the exquisitely furnished wood-panelled cabin of King Carlos and Queen Amélia from the royal yacht Amélia, built in Scotland in 1900.

The modern, incongruous pavilion opposite houses original royal barges, the most extravagant of which is the royal brig built in 1780 for Maria I. The collection ends with an exhibition of seaplanes, including the Santa Clara, which made the first crossing of the South Atlantic, from Lisbon to Rio de Janeiro, in 1922.

VASCO DA GAMA (C 1460–1524)

In 1498, Vasco da Gama (right) sailed around the Cape of Good Hope and opened the sea route to India. Although the Hindu ruler of Calicut was not excited by his humble offerings of cloth and wash basins, Da Gama returned to Portugal with a cargo of spices. In 1502, he sailed again to India, setting up Portuguese trade routes in the Indian Ocean. João III nominated him viceroy of India in 1524, but he died soon after.

---

⑨

Centro Cultural de Belém

📍 B9 🏛 Praça do Império
🚌 714, 727, 728, 729, 751
🚊 15 🚆 Belém ⏰ 8am–8pm
Mon–Fri, 10am–6pm Sat,
Sun & public hols 🌐 ccb.pt

Standing between the Tagus and the Jerónimos monastery, this stark, modern building was erected as the headquarters of the Portuguese presidency of the European Community. In 1993 it opened as a cultural centre offering performing arts, music and photography. An exhibition centre houses the Museu Colecção Berardo (p123).

Both the café and restaurant spill out onto the ramparts of the building, whose peaceful gardens look out over the quay and the river.

---

⑩

Padrão dos Descobrimentos

📍 C10 🏛 Avenida de Brasília 🚌 727, 728 🚊 15
🚆 Belém ⏰ Mar–Sep: 10am–7pm daily; Oct–Feb: 10am–6pm Tue–Sun 🚫 1 Jan, 1 May, 25 Dec 🌐 padraodos descobrimentos.pt

Standing prominently on the Belém waterfront, this huge angular structure, the Padrão dos Descobrimentos (Monument to the Discoveries), was built in 1960 to mark the 500th anniversary of the death of Henry the Navigator. The 52-m- (170-ft-) high monument, commissioned by the Salazar regime, commemorates the mariners, royal patrons and all those who took part in the development of the Portuguese Age of Discovery. The monument is designed in the shape of a caravel, with Portugal's coat of arms on the sides and the sword of the Royal House of Avis rising above the entrance. Henry the Navigator stands at the prow with a caravel in hand. In two sloping lines either side of the monument are stone statues of Portuguese heroes linked with the Age of Discovery, such as Dom Manuel I holding an armillary sphere, the poet Camões with a copy of *Os Lusíadas* and the painter Nuno Gonçalves.

On the monument's north side, the huge mariner's compass cut into the paving stone was a gift from South Africa in 1960. The central map, dotted with galleons and mermaids, shows the routes of the discoverers in the 15th and 16th centuries. Inside the monument, a lift (there is a fee) whisks you up to the sixth floor where steps then lead to the top for a splendid panorama of Belém. The basement level is used for temporary exhibitions.

The Padrão is not to everyone's taste but the setting is undeniably splendid and the caravel design is imaginative. The monument looks particularly dramatic when viewed from the west in the light of the late afternoon sun.

11

Museu Colecção Berardo

📍 B9 🏛 Praça do Império
🚌 727, 728, 729, 751 🚊 15
🚉 Belém 🕐 10am–7pm daily 🌐 museuberardo.pt

The brainchild of business mogul and art collector José Manuel Rodrigues Berardo, this fascinating gallery, in the Centro Cultural de Belém, boasts around 1,000 works by more than 500 artists. The Museu Colecção Berardo provides a rich compendium

of a century of modern and contemporary art through a variety of media, from canvas to sculpture and from photography to video installations.

Highlights include Pablo Picasso's *Tête de Femme* (1909), a good example of the Spanish artist's Cubist style; variants of Andy Warhol's famous *Brillo Box* (1964–8); and Jeff Koons' *Poodle* (1991). Other artists on show include Francis Bacon, Willem de Kooning and Henry Moore. Notable Portuguese art on display includes Alberto Carneiro's sculptures and etchings by Paula Rego.

← Padrão dos Descobrimentos, inaugurated in 1960

The imposing Padrão dos Descobrimentos, dominating Belém's waterfront

MAAT - Museu de Arte, Arquitetura e Tecnologia

📍D9 🏠Avenida Brasília
🚍727, 728, 729 🚊15
🚋Belém 🕐11-7pm Wed-Mon 🚫1 Jan,
1 May & 25 Dec 🌐maat.pt

With riverside views, the stylish Museu de Arte, Arquitetura e Tecnologia, popularly known as MAAT, is operated by the EDP Foundation, and is dedicated to contemporary art, primarily Portuguese, along with modern architecture and technology. Exhibits are housed in an award-winning building designed by the London-based architect Amanda Levete. Its structure is a sharp contrast to the well-known Lisbon power station, which stands next door and forms an integral part of this building complex. Visits to the MAAT include a tour of the iconic power station, and access to the building's undulating pedestrian roof which affords stunning views of Lisbon and the Tagus river.

As well as cutting-edge temporary exhibitions, the museum also features the Pedro Cabrita Reis Collection, which consists of some 400 works by over 70 artists from the end of the 20th century.

↑ Colourful stained glass gracing the chapel of Ermida de São Jerónimo

Ermida de São Jerónimo

📍A8 🏠Praça de Itália
📞210 966 989 🚍714, 728, 729, 732, 751 🕐Mon-Sat (by appointment only)

Also known as the Capela de São Jerónimo, this little chapel was constructed in 1514 when Diogo Boitac was working on the Jerónimos monastery (p116). Although a far simpler building, it is also Manueline in style and may have been

built to a design by Boitac. The only decorative elements on the monolithic chapel are the four pinnacles, corner gargoyles and Manueline portal. Perched on a quiet hill above Belém, the chapel has fine views. A path from the terrace winds down the hill towards the Torre de Belém.

Igreja da Memória

📍C8 🏠Calçada do Galvão, Ajuda 📞213 635 295 🚍728, 732 🚊18 🕐For Mass: 6pm Mon-Sat, 10am Sun

Built in 1760, this church was founded by King José I in gratitude for his escape from an assassination plot on the site in 1758. The king was returning from a secret liaison with a lady of the noble Távora family when his carriage was attacked and a bullet hit him in the arm. Pombal (p138) used this as an excuse to get rid of his enemies in the Távora family,

MAAT, housed in an innovative building ↓ beside the Tagus river

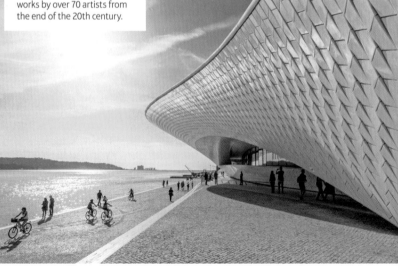

↑ Manicured formal gardens of the Jardim Botânico da Ajuda

accusing them of conspiracy. In 1759 they were savagely tortured and executed. Their deaths are commemorated by a pillar in Beco do Chão Salgado, off Rua de Belém.

The Neo-Classical domed church has a marble-clad interior and a small chapel, on the right, containing the tomb of Pombal, who died at the age of 83, a year after being banished from Lisbon.

Jardim Botânico da Ajuda

📍C7 🏛Calçada da Ajuda
🚌714, 727, 728, 729, 732
🚋18 🕙9am-6pm daily
(to 8pm May-Sep) 🚫1 Jan,
25 Dec 🌐isa.ulisboa.pt/jba

Laid out on two levels by Pombal in 1768, these

> 💬 INSIDER TIP
> **Plan(t) Ahead**
>
> To view the most exotic plant specimens in the Jardim Botânico da Ajuda, head straight for the upper level. Here you can delight at the ancient dragon tree from Madeira and a sprawling Schotia Afra.

Italian-style gardens provide a pleasant respite from the noisy suburbs of Belém. The entrance on Calçada da Ajuda (wrought-iron gates in a pink wall) is easy to miss. The park comprises 5,000 plant species from Africa, Asia and America. Notable features are the 400-year-old dragon tree, native of Madeira, and the flamboyant 18th-century fountain decorated with serpents, winged fish, sea horses and mythical creatures. A majestic terrace looks out over the lower level of the gardens.

Palácio Nacional da Ajuda

📍D7 🏛Largo da Ajuda
🚌732, 742, 760 🚋18
🕙10am-5:30pm Thu-Tue
(last adm 5pm) 🚫1 Jan,
Easter, 1 May, 13 Jun, 25 Dec
🌐palacioajuda.gov.pt

The royal palace, which was destroyed by fire in 1795, was replaced in the early 19th century by this magnificent Neo-Classical building set around a large quadrangle. It was left incomplete when the royal family was forced into exile in Brazil in 1807, following the invasion of Portugal.

€20 million

The cost of building the spectacular Museu de Arte, Arquitetura e Tecnologia.

The palace only became a permanent residence of the royal family when Luís I became king in 1861 and married an Italian Princess, Maria Pia di Savoia. No expense was spared in furnishing the apartments, which are decorated with silk wallpaper, Sèvres porcelain and crystal chandeliers.

A prime example of regal excess is the extraordinary Saxe Room, a wedding present to Maria Pia from the King of Saxony, in which every piece of furniture is decorated with Meissen porcelain. On the first floor, the huge Banqueting Hall, with crystal chandeliers, silk-covered chairs and an allegory of the birth of João VI on the frescoed ceiling, is truly impressive. At the other end of the palace, Luís I's Neo-Gothic painting studio is a more intimate display of intricately carved furniture.

A SHORT WALK
BELÉM

Distance 1.5 km (1 mile) **Nearest station** Mosteiro dos Jerónimos tram stop **Time** 25 minutes

Portugal's former maritime glory, expressed in imposing, exuberant buildings such as the Jerónimos monastery, is evident everywhere in Belém. Silted up since the days of the caravels, this picturesque area along the waterfront was restructured at Salazar's (p55) insistence, in an attempt to revive awareness of and celebrate the country's Golden Age. A stroll here is consequently littered with historically signi-ficant sights: Praça do Império was laid out for the 1940 Exhibition of the Portuguese World, while Praça Afonso de Albuquerque was dedicated to Portugal's first viceroy of India. The Palácio de Belém, restored in the 18th century, briefly housed the royal family after the earthquake of 1755.

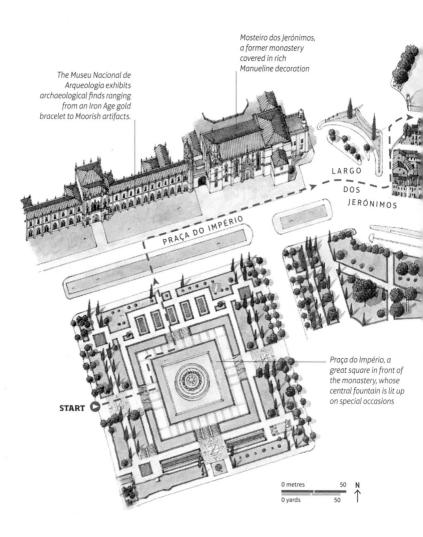

The Museu Nacional de Arqueologia exhibits archaeological finds ranging from an Iron Age gold bracelet to Moorish artifacts.

Mosteiro dos Jerónimos, a former monastery covered in rich Manueline decoration

LARGO
DOS
JERÓNIMOS

PRAÇA DO IMPÉRIO

Praça do Império, a great square in front of the monastery, whose central fountain is lit up on special occasions

START

0 metres   50
0 yards   50

N ↑

↑ The vaulted arcades of the Manueline cloister of Mosteiro dos Jerónimos

Locator Map
For more detail see p114

Jardim Botânico Tropical, peaceful gardens filled with exotic plants and trees gathered from Portugal's former colonies

Palácio de Belém, a former royal palace that is now the residence of the Portuguese president

TRAVESSA DOS FERREIROS

T. MARIA PINTO

◯ **FINISH**

RUA DE BELÉM

RUA VIEIRA PORTUENSE

Stop at Antiga Confeitaria de Belém, the birthplace of pastéis de Belém (rich custard tarts).

Rua Vieira Portuense is lined with colourful 16th- and 17th-century houses and runs alongside a small park.

Praça Afonso de Albuquerque, a public square with a central Neo-Manueline statue of the first Portuguese viceroy of India, after whom the space is named

Did You Know?

Manuel I granted the Mosteiro dos Jerónimos to the Hieronymite order, said to protect kings after death.

The Cristo Rei sculpture glimpsed through the red towers of the Ponte 25 de Abril

Must Sees

1. Museu Calouste Gulbenkian
2. Museu Nacional do Azulejo

Experience More

3. Praça Marquês de Pombal
4. Cristo Rei
5. Parque Eduardo VII
6. Ponte 25 de Abril
7. Doca de Santo Amaro
8. Fundação Oriente Museu
9. Museu da Carris
10. LX Factory
11. Campo Pequeno
12. Museo da Água
13. Parque das Nações
14. Oceanário de Lisboa
15. Museu de Lisboa
16. Aqueduto das Águas Livres
17. Palácio Fronteira
18. Parque do Monteiro-Mor

BEYOND THE CENTRE

Away from the city centre, Lisbon unfolds in a blend of residential sprawl, industrial parks and the remnants of ancient villages. Older sights include the manicured Parque Eduardo VII to the north, and the 16th-century, tile-fronted Palácio Fronteira to the northwest.

Most of Lisbon's outlying suburbs originated more recently, however, with several Salazar-era buildings and structures – such as the vast Cristo Rei – springing up during the mid-20th century.

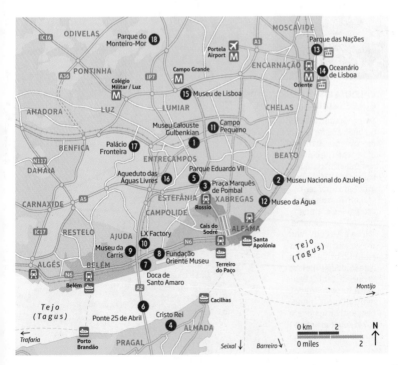

❶ 🖫 🍴 🖥 🛍

MUSEU CALOUSTE GULBENKIAN

🏠 Avenida de Berna 45A 🚌 713, 716, 726, 742, 746, 756 Ⓜ Praça de Espanha or São Sebastião ⏰ 10am–6pm Wed–Mon (free Sun after 2pm) ⛔ 1 Jan, Easter, 1 May, 24 & 25 Dec 🌐 gulbenkian.pt/museu

Thanks to wealthy Armenian oil magnate Calouste Gulbenkian's wide-ranging tastes and his eye for a masterpiece, this museum has one of the finest collections of art in Europe.

The museum's works are split across two separately housed collections, linked by a serene stretch of urban park. The Founder's Collection – Gulbenkian's personal pieces – sits within a purpose-built museum dating from 1969, with varied exhibits ranging from ancient Egyptian statuettes to an astonishing array of René Lalique Art Nouveau jewellery. South of the gardens stands the Modern Collection, widely considered to be the world's most complete collection of modern Portuguese art. Standard tickets allow access to both collections, while the sculpture-dotted gardens can be explored free of charge.

CALOUSTE GULBENKIAN

Born in Scutari in 1869, Gulbenkian started his art collection at the age of 14, when he bought some ancient coins in a bazaar. In 1928, he was granted a 5 per cent stake in four major oil companies, earning himself the nickname "Mr Five Per Cent". With the wealth he accumulated, Gulbenkian was able to indulge his love of fine art. During World War II, he went to live in neutral Portugal, and bequeathed his estate to his adopted nation upon his death in 1955.

6,000

The approximate number of artworks Gulbenkian amassed in his personal collection.

1. The blocky concrete building in which the Founder's Collection is housed.

2. This fine marble statue of Diana, goddess of the hunt, is part of the Founder's Collection.

3. The spacious galleries of the Founder's Collection.

1

2

3

↑ Exhibits within the museum's extensive Modern Collection

FOUNDER'S COLLECTION

Ranking alongside the Museu de Arte Antiga *(p96)* as the finest museum in Lisbon, the Founder's Collection exhibits, which span over 4,000 years from ancient Egyptian figurines, through translucent Islamic glassware, to Art Nouveau brooches, are displayed in spacious and well-lit galleries, many overlooking the gardens or courtyards. Although the museum is not large, each work of art is worthy of attention.

In the Egyptian, Classical and Mesopotamian gallery priceless treasures chart the evolution of Egyptian art from the Old Kingdom (c 2700 BC) to the Roman Period (from the 1st century BC). Outstanding pieces in the Classical art section include a magnificent redfigure Greek vase, and a Roman satyr's head from the 2nd century AD.

The museum's Eastern art is also remarkable. Being Armenian, Gulbenkian had a keen interest in works from the Near and Middle East, resulting in a fine collection of Persian and Turkish carpets, textiles, costumes and ceramics in the Oriental Islamic gallery. In terms of Far Eastern pieces, there is a large collection of Chinese porcelain acquired by Gulbenkian between 1907 and 1947. One of the rarest pieces is a small blue-glazed bowl from the Yuan Dynasty (1271–1368). The carefully plotted route around the

↑ Rembrandt's *Portrait of an Old Man* (1645), a masterclass in light and shade

museum ends with a room filled with the flamboyant Art Nouveau creations of French jeweller René Lalique (1860–1945). Gulbenkian was a close friend of Lalique's and acquired many of the pieces on display directly from the artist. Inlaid with semiprecious stones and covered with enamel or gold leaf, the ornate collection constitutes a spectacular finish to this unique and incredibly diverse museum.

← Porcelain vases on display within the Founder's Collection

Visitor wandering the galleries of the Founder's Collection ↑

FOUNDER'S COLLECTION PIECES

St Catherine
A serene 15th-century bust, painted by the Flemish artist Rogier van der Weyden.

Boy Blowing Bubbles
Édouard Manet's 1867 painting considers the transience of life and art.

Yuan Dynasty Stem Cup
This blue-glazed piece is decorated with delicate reliefs of Taoist figures under bamboo leaves.

Diana Statue
A graceful marble statue *(p133)*, once owned by Catherine the Great and considered too obscene to exhibit.

Ancient Greek Vase
This 5th century BC vase is adorned with mythological motifs.

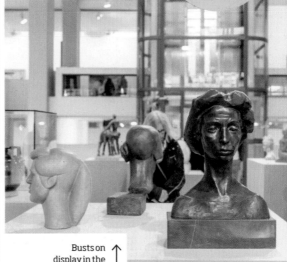

Busts on display in the Modern Collection ↑

MODERN COLLECTION

The Modern Collection lies across the gardens from the Founder's Collection and is part of the same cultural foundation. It is housed in a large, light-filled building, designed by architect Sir Leslie Martin in 1983.

The permanent collection features over 10,000 works, with an emphasis on paintings and sculpture by Portuguese artists from the turn of the 20th century to the present day. Perhaps the most famous painting is the striking portrait of poet Fernando Pessoa in the Café Irmãos Unidos (1964) by José de Almada Negreiros (1893–1970), a leading exponent of Portuguese Modernism. The oil painting was commissioned by the Calouste Gulbenkian Foundation, and intended to replicate a similar portrait that Almada had produced for the café itself.

Also of interest are paintings by Eduardo Viana (1881–1967), Amadeo de Sousa Cardoso (1887–1910) and contemporary artists such as Rui Sanches, Graça Morais, Teresa Magalhães

and – perhaps the best known – Paula Rego. Rego settled in London in the mid-1970s, but she has long been hailed in Portugal as one of the nation's greatest living artists. Her work often contains elements of magical realism, although later works have gradually tended towards more realistic renderings.

Within the international collection are works by big hitters such as David Hockney and British sculptor Antony Gormley (renowned for his *Angel of the North* sculpture in Gateshead, England).

As well as the exhibition space, which comprises three linked galleries, there is also an events area, a busy café and a museum bookshop.

Did You Know?

Paula Rego's pieces have fetched up to £1.1 million at auction, a record for a Portuguese artist.

PICTURE PERFECT
Manueline Designs

Set around a central courtyard, the cloister is a serene spot. Its delicate columns and carved vaulted walkways are the perfect place to point your lens.

MUSEU NACIONAL DO AZULEJO

⌂ Rua da Madre de Deus 4 🚌 718, 728, 742, 759, 794 🕐 10am-6pm Tue-Sun
🕐 Mon, public hols 🌐 museudoazulejo.gov.pt

Housed in a beautiful 16th-century convent, the National Tile Museum offers an unmatched display of this uniquely Portuguese art form, with *azulejos* dating from the 15th century right through to the present day.

Dona Leonor, widow of King João II, founded the Convento da Madre de Deus in 1509. Built in Manueline style, restorations of the church under João III and João V added its simple Renaissance designs and striking Baroque decoration. The stunning convent cloisters are now home to the National Tile Museum. Decorative panels and individual tiles trace the evolution of tile-making from its Moorish roots up to the current Portuguese art form. The walls of the restaurant are lined with 19th-century tiles, depicting hanging game, from wild boar and pheasants to fish.

Did You Know?

The word *azulejo* has Arabic roots - it means "small polished stone".

↑ Fine 17th-century tiles patterning the cloister from the original convent

① The church's Manueline portal was recreated from a 16th-century painting.

② The 16th-century church of Madre de Deus acquired its sumptuous interiors under João V. The Rococo altarpiece was added after the earthquake of 1755.

③ On the top floor, a striking 18th-century panorama depicts Lisbon before the 1755 earthquake.

EXPERIENCE MORE

❸

Praça Marquês de Pombal

🚌 711, 712, 720 & many other routes Ⓜ Marquês de Pombal

At the top of Avenida da Liberdade (p84), traffic thunders round the "Rotunda" (roundabout), as the *praça* is also known. At the centre is a lofty 1934 monument to Pombal. The despotic states-man, who virtually ruled Portugal from 1750 to 1777, stands on the top of the column, his hand on a lion (a symbol of power) and his eyes directed down to the Baixa, whose creation he masterminded. Allegorical images depicting Pombal's political, educational and agricultural reforms decorate the base of the monument. Although greatly feared, this dynamic politician propelled the country into the Age of Enlightenment. Broken blocks of stone at the foot of the monument and tidal waves flooding the city are an allegory of the destruction caused by the 1755 earthquake.

Nearby, the well-tended Parque Eduardo VII (p139) extends northwards behind the square. The paving stones around the Rotunda are dec-orated with a mosaic of Lisbon's coat of arms. Many of the city's sightseeing operators have their main

pick-up located at the bottom of Parque Eduardo VII. There is also a multilingual booth where visitors can buy tickets and plan excursions.

---

❹

Cristo Rei

🏠 Santuário Nacional do Cristo Rei, Alto do Pragal, Almada 🚢 from Cais do Sodré to Cacilhas then 🚌 101 🕐 9:30am-6pm daily (to 6:45pm Jul-Sep) 🌐 cristorei.pt

Modelled on the Cristo Redentor in Rio de Janeiro (Brazil), this giant-sized statue stands with arms outstretched on the south bank of the Tagus river. The impressive 28-m- (92-ft-) tall figure of Christ, mounted on an 82-m (269-ft) pedestal, was sculpted by Francisco Franco in 1949–59 at the instigation of Prime Minister Salazar.

You can see the monument from various viewpoints in the city, but it is fun to take a ferry from Cais do Sodré to the Margem Sul (the south bank, which until recently was usually simply known as the Outra Banda, or "other bank"), then a bus or taxi to the monument. A lift plus some

↑ The mammoth Cristo Rei statue, soaring high into the sky

💬 **INSIDER TIP**
River Views

Take the passenger ferry from Cais do Sodré across the Tagus to the little port of Cacilhas, where you'll find many riverfront seafood restaurants and great views of Lisbon back across the water.

↑ Expansive views of the city from the *miradouro* of Parque Eduardo VII

steps take you up 82 m (269 ft) to the top of the pedestal, affording fine views of the city and river below.

---

5 ⬨ ▭

Parque Eduardo VII

🏛 Praça Marquês de Pombal
📞 213 882 278 🚌 711, 712, 720 Ⓜ Marquês de Pombal
🕐 Estufa Fria: 10am-7pm daily (Nov-Mar: 9am-5pm)
🚫 1 Jan, 1 May, 25 Dec

Central Lisbon's largest park was named after King Edward VII of the United Kingdom, who came to Lisbon in 1902 to reaffirm the Anglo-Portuguese alliance.

The wide grassy slope, which extends for 25 hectares (62 acres), was laid out as Parque da Liberdade, a continuation of Avenida da Liberdade (p84), in the late 19th century. Neatly clipped box hedging, flanked by mosaic patterned walkways, stretches uphill from the Praça Marquês de Pombal to a belvedere at the top. Here you will find a flower-filled garden dedicated to the memory of renowned Portuguese *fado* singer Amália Rodrigues, and

a pleasant café. The vantage point at the summit of the park offers fine, sweeping views of the city. On clear days you can see as far as the Serra da Arrábida, a nature reserve located 40km (25 miles) from the city centre (p167).

Situated in the northwest corner, the most inspiring feature of this park is the jungle-like Estufa Fria, or greenhouse, where exotic plants, streams and waterfalls provide serene respite from the city streets. At this urban oasis there are in fact three greenhouses: in the Estufa Fria (cold greenhouse), palms push through the slatted bamboo roof and paths wind through a forest of ferns, fuchsias, flowering shrubs and banana trees; the warmer Estufa Quente and Estufa Doce are filled with tropical plants, water-lily ponds and impressive cacti.

Near the *estufas*, a pond with carp and a galleon-shaped play area are popular with children. On the east side, the Pavilhão Carlos Lopes, named after the 1984 Olympic marathon winner, was extensively refurbished in 2016 and is now used for concerts, exhibitions and conferences.

↑ Ponte 25 de Abril
illuminated at night, with
the city lights behind

6

Ponte 25 de Abril

🚌 753

Once called the Ponte Salazar after the dictator who had it built in 1966, Lisbon's suspension bridge was renamed to commemorate the revolution of 25 April 1974 that restored democracy to Portugal (p55).

Inspired by San Francisco's Golden Gate Bridge in the US, this steel construction stretches for 2 km (1 mile). The lower tier was modified in 1999 to accommodate the Fertagus, a railway across the Tagus. The bridge's notorious traffic congestion has been partly resolved by the opening of the 17-km (11-mile) Vasco da Gama bridge. Spanning the Tagus river from Montijo to Sacavém, north of the Parque das Nações, this bridge was completed in 1998.

7

Doca de Santo Amaro

🚌 714, 727, 732, 751, 756
🚋 15 🚇 Alcântara-Mar

In the early 1930s, Lisbon's docks at Alcântara were the city's main access point. As the importance of the docks declined, the once-industrial riverside has been opened up.

One of the best places to head for is the Doca de Santo Amaro, a largely enclosed dock that sits below the humming traffic of the dramatic Ponte 25 de Abril. The inner edge of the docks is lined with former warehouses, converted in the 1990s and now housing cafés, restaurants and bars with fine views over the water. These tend to be popular, and tables on the outside terraces get snapped up quickly.

Beneath the bridge to the west of the docks is a strange,

↓ Brisé fan from China
  in the Fundação
↓ Oriente Museu

GREAT VIEW
Ponte 25 de Abril

For a unique experience take the lift up Pillar 7 of this landmark bridge, which offers unbroken views across the river and the city's south bank from 80 m (262 ft) above the waves. Tickets cost around €6.

boomerang-shaped structure, designed to stop falling debris. Continue past this and it's a good 20-minute walk to Belém.

---

8 🔶 🍴 🖥 🛍

Fundação Oriente Museu

📍 Avenida Brasília, Doca de Alcântara Norte 🚌712, 714, 728, 738, 742 ⏰10am-6pm Tue-Sun (to 10pm Fri) 🌐museudooriente.pt

This museum and cultural centre is dedicated to showing the historical and cultural links between Portugal and its former colonies in the East.

The permanent exhibition is split into two collections. The Portuguese Presence in Asia has a selection of exhibits ranging from furniture and jewellery to porcelain, paintings and textiles. Highlights include 17th- and 18th-century Chinese and Japanese folding screens and some rare examples of Namban art – Portuguese-influenced Japanese art of the 16th and 17th centuries.

The second exhibition is the Kwok On Collection, which features the performing arts of a vast geographic area extending from Turkey to Japan. It includes fine masks from Asia and a section on shadow and puppet theatre from India, China and Indonesia.

---

9 🔶 🛍

Museu da Carris

📍 Rua 1 de Maiao 🚌714, 727, 732 ⏰10am-6pm Tue-Sat 🌐museu.carris.pt

Carris is the company that runs Lisbon's surface public transport and this museum details the history of a system that has had to negotiate a broad river estuary and some serious hills since 1872.

Set in a sprawling former tram depot, the museum is divided into three zones. The first uses various exhibits to

trace the development of Lisbon's public transport. You can then take a fun trip on a tram to the other two zones, which are filled with historic trams and buses, including early horse-drawn varieties.

Down by the river at the bottom of the site, a collection of old shipping containers and double-decker buses make up Village Underground, an innovative work space for Lisbon's creative set.

---

10 🍴 🖥 🛍

LX Factory

📍 Rua Rodrigues Faria 103 🚌201, 742, 751, 756, 760 🌐lxfactory.com

Virtually beneath the Ponte 25 de Abril in a slightly shabby part of town, LX Factory is one of the hippest places in Lisbon. The complex is inside a huge former textiles plant, with the warehouses, factory spaces and courtyards transformed into studios and workshops for the arts, fashion and creative media. Woven among them are innovative cafés, bars, restaurants and shops. Visit on Sunday morning when a lively flea market takes place.

Shelves stacked to the ceiling at Ler Devagar bookshop in LX Factory ↑

Ponte 25 de Abril and Cristo Rei, as seen from one of the LX Factory's buzzing bars

Neo-Moorish façade
of the bullring in
Campo Pequeno

Campo Pequeno

🚌 736, 744 Ⓜ Campo
🕐 Pequeno Bullring: 10am-
11pm daily

This square is dominated by
the red-brick Neo-Moorish
bullring built in the late 19th
century. The building has
undergone development, and
a car park and leisure centre
have been added. Much of
the bullring's distinctive
architecture, such as keyhole-
shaped windows and double
cupolas, have been retained.

Museu da Água

🏛 Rua do Alviela 12 📞 218
100 215 🚌 735 🕐 10am-
5:30pm daily 🚫 Public hols

Dedicated to the history of
Lisbon's water supply, this
informative museum was
imaginatively created around
the city's first steam pumping
station. It commemorates
Manuel da Maia, the 18th-
century engineer behind the
Águas Livres aqueduct (p146).
    Pride of place goes to four
lovingly preserved steam
engines, one of which still
functions (by electricity). The
development of technology
relating to the city's water

supply is documented with
photographs. Particularly
interesting is the exhibit on
the Alfama's 17th-century
Chafariz d'El Rei, one of
Lisbon's first fountains. Locals
used to queue at one of six
founts, depending on their
social status.

Parque das Nações

🏛 Avenida Dom João ll
🚌 705, 725, 728, 744, 750,
782 Ⓜ Oriente 🚆 Oriente
🕐 Park: 24 hours daily;
Pavilhão do Conhecimento:
10am-6pm Tue-Fri, 11am-
7pm Sat & Sun 🚫 1 Jan, 24,
25 & 31 Dec 🌐 portaldas
nacoes.pt

Originally the site of Expo 98,
Parque das Nações is now a
Lisbon hub. With its contemporary architecture and
family-oriented attractions,
the park has renewed the
eastern waterfront, which was
once an industrial wasteland.
The soaring geometry of
the platform canopies over
Santiago Calatrava's Oriente
Station set the architectural
tone. The Portugal Pavilion
has a large reinforced concrete
roof suspended like a sailcloth
above its forecourt.
    Pavilhão do Conhecimento –
Ciencia Viva is a fascinating

Did You Know?

The Vasco da Gama
bridge (near the Parque
das Nações) is Europe's
longest, stretching
17 km (11 miles).

modern museum of science
and technology that houses
several interactive exhibitions.
    Spectacular views can be
had from the cable car that
links the Torre Vasco da
Gama with the marina. The
promenade along the river
also offers delightful views,
including of the Vasco da
Gama bridge. Also in the
area is the MEO Arena.

Oceanário de Lisboa

🏛 Esplanada Dom Carlos 1,
Parque das Nações 🚌 705,
725, 728, 744, 750, 782
Ⓜ Oriente 🚆 Oriente
🕐 10am-8pm daily (to 7pm
Nov-Mar) 🌐 oceanario.pt

The main attraction at Parque
das Nações, the oceanarium
was designed by American
architect Peter Chermayeff,
and is perched on the end of

> The aquarium's vast central tank has a dazzling variety of fish, large and small. Sharks co-exist peaceably with bream in the softly lit waters.

a pier. It holds an impressive array of species – birds and some mammals as well as fish and other underwater dwellers.

Landscapes represent the habitats of the Atlantic, Pacific, Indian and Antarctic oceans, with suitable fauna and flora. The aquarium's vast central tank has a dazzling variety of fish, large and small. Sharks co-exist peaceably with bream in the softly lit waters.

15

Museu de Lisboa

🏛 Campo Grande 245
🚌 736, 747, 750 Ⓜ Campo Grande 🕙 10am-6pm Tue-Sun 🚫 1 Jan, 1 May, 25 Dec
🌐 museudelisboa.pt

Palácio Pimenta was allegedly commissioned by João V for his mistress Madre Paula, a nun from the nearby convent at Odivelas. When the mansion was built, in the middle of the 18th century, it occupied a

Visitors watching the fish in the central tank at Oceanário de Lisboa ↓

peaceful site outside the city. Nowadays it has to contend with the traffic of Campo Grande. The house itself, however, retains its period charm.

The displays follow the development of the city, from prehistoric times through the Romans, Visigoths and Moors, traced by means of drawings tiles, paintings, models and historical documents. Notable exhibits are those depicting the city before the earthquake of 1755, including a highly detailed model made in the 1950s and an impressive 17th- century oil painting by Dirk Stoop (1610–86) of *Terreiro do Paço*, as Praça do Comércio was known then *(p80)*. One room is devoted to the Águas Livres aqueduct *(p146)*, with architectural plans as well as prints and watercolours of the completed aqueduct.

The earthquake theme is resumed with pictures of the city amid the devastation and various plans for its reconstruction. The museum brings you into the 20th century with a large colour poster celebrating the Revolution of 1910 and the proclamation of the new republic *(p55)*.

EAT

Eleven
Michelin-star dining and stunning city views are on offer at this airy, modern restaurant. Opt for an à la carte or a tasting menu - or the lavish lobster menu, comprised wholly of the freshest shellfish.

🏛 Rua Marquês da Fronteira, Jardim Amália Rodrigues
🚫 Sun 🌐 restaurant eleven.com

€€€

O Farol
This centuries-old establishment is the best-known seafood restaurant in Cacilhas. Diners come here to delight in the tanks filled with lobsters, great views across the Tagus river and fine-tasting beer.

🏛 Alfredo Dinis Alex 1-3, Cacilhas
🌐 restaurantefarol.com

€€€

Pastelaria Versailles
A wonderful array of cakes and pastries are on offer at this traditional café, which dates from the early 1920s. Good-value lunches are also served, while the decadent, cream-topped hot chocolate makes a tasty treat on chilly afternoons.

🏛 Avenida da República 15a, Saldanha
📞 213 546 340

€€€

Imposing arches of the Aqueduto das Águas Livres ↑

16 🖼️

Aqueduto das Águas Livres

🏛️ Best seen from Calçada da Quintinha 🚌 774, 783 🕐 10am–5:30pm Tue–Sun; Mãe d'Água das Amoreiras: 10am–12:30pm, 1:30–5:30 Tue–Sun 🚫 Public hols

Considered the most beautiful sight in Lisbon at the turn of the 20th century, the impressive structure of Aqueduto das Águas Livres looms over the Alcântara valley northwest of the city. The construction of an aqueduct gave João V (p54) the opportunity to indulge his passion for grandiose building schemes, as the only area of Lisbon with fresh drinking water was the Alfama. A tax on meat, wine, olive oil and other comestibles funded the project, and although not complete until the 19th century, it was already supplying the city with water by 1748. The main pipeline measures 19 km (12 miles), but the total length,

Did You Know?

Aqueduto das Águas Livres only stopped supplying water for human consumption in the 1960s.

including all the secondary channels, is 58 km (36 miles). The most visible part of this imposing structure are the 35 arches crossing the Alcântara valley, the tallest of which rise to 65 m (213 ft) above ground.

It is possible to take guided tours over the Alcântara arches. There are also tours of the Mãe d'Água reservoir and trips to the Mãe d'Água springs. Contact the Museu da Água (p144) for details of the trips.

At the end of the aqueduct, the Mãe d'Água das Amoreiras is a castle-like building that served as a reservoir for the water supplied from the aqueduct. Today the space is used for art exhibitions, fashion shows and other events.

---

17 🖼️ 🖼️

Palácio Fronteira

🏛️ Largo São Domingos de Benfica 1 📞 217 782 023 🚌 770 Ⓜ️ Jardim Zoológico 🏛️ Benfica 🕐 By tour only Jun–Sep: 10:30, 11am, 11:30am, noon; Oct–May: 11am, noon 🚫 Sun, public hols

This country manor house was built as a hunting pavilion for João de Mascarenhas, the first Marquês de Fronteira, in 1640. Although skyscrapers are visible in the distance, it still occupies a quiet spot, by the Parque Florestal de Monsanto.

Both house and garden have *azulejo* decoration whose subjects include battle scenes and trumpet-blowing monkeys.

Although the palace is still occupied by the 12th marquis, some of the living rooms and the library, as well as the formal gardens, are included in the tour. The Battles Room has lively tiled panels depicting scenes of the War of Restoration (1640–68), with a detail of João de Fronteira fighting a Spanish general. It was his loyalty to Pedro II during this war that earned him the title of Marquês. Interesting comparisons can be made between these naive 17th-century Portuguese tiles and the Delft ones from the same period in the dining room, depicting naturalistic scenes. The dining room is also decorated with frescoed panels and portraits of Portuguese nobility.

The late-16th-century chapel is the oldest part of the house. The façade is adorned with stones, shells, broken glass and bits of china. These fragments of crockery are believed to have been used at the feast inaugurating the

INSIDER TIP
Catch a Match

Two of Europe's leading football clubs play in Lisbon: Sporting Lisbon launched the career of Cristiano Ronaldo, while Benfica have two European Cups to their name. Tickets can be bought at the stadiums or online.

palace and then smashed to ensure no one else could sup off the same set. Visits to the garden start at the chapel terrace, where tiled niches are decorated with figures personifying the arts and mythological creatures.

In the formal Italian garden the immaculate box hedges are cut into shapes to represent the seasons of the year. To one end, tiled scenes of dashing knights on horseback, representing ancestors of the Fronteira family, are reflected in the waters of a large tank. On either side of the water, a grand staircase leads to a terrace above. Here, decorative niches contain the busts of Portuguese kings and

colourful majolica reliefs adorn the arcades. More blue-and-white tiled scenes, realistic and allegorical, decorate the wall at the far end of the garden.

Parque do Monteiro-Mor

📍Largo Júlio Castilho 📞217 567 620 🚌703, 736, 796 Ⓜ️Lumiar 🕐Park: 2-6pm Tue, 10am-10pm Wed-Sun

Monteiro-Mor park was sold to the state in 1975 and the 18th-century palace buildings were converted to museums. The gardens are attractive; much of the land is wooded, though the area around the museums has gardens with flowering shrubs, duck ponds and tropical trees.

The slightly old-fashioned **Museu Nacional do Traje**

(Costume Museum) has a vast collection of textiles, accessories and costumes worn by people of note.

The **Museu Nacional do Teatro** has two buildings: one devoted to temporary exhibitions, the other containing a small permanent collection. Photographs, posters and cartoons feature famous 20th-century Portuguese actors, and one section is devoted to Amália Rodrigues, the famous *fado* singer (p43).

Museu Nacional do Traje
🕐2-6pm Tue, 10am-6pm Wed-Sun 🌐museu dotraje.gov.pt

Museu Nacional do Teatro
🕐10am-6pm Tue-Sun 🔒1 Jan, Easter, 1 May, 25 Dec 🌐museudoteatro edanca.gov.pt

Tiled terrace, decorated with figures *(inset)*, leading to the chapel of the Palácio Fronteira ↓

THE LISBON COAST

Within an hour's drive northwest of Lisbon you can reach Portugal's rocky Atlantic coast. Traders and invaders, from the Phoenicians to the Spanish, have left their mark on this region – in particular the Moors, whose forts and castles, rebuilt many times over the centuries, can be found all along the coast. After Lisbon became the country's capital in 1256, Portuguese kings and nobles built summer palaces and villas in the countryside west of the city, and on the cool, green heights of the Serra de Sintra. Along the "Portuguese Riviera", wealthy Lisboetas have been building holiday villas in the seaside resort of Cascais as far back as the late 19th century.

Neighbouring Estoril became fashionable when exiled European royalty moved there during World War II; in its heyday, the town became a hotbed for spies, including Ian Fleming, who recreated Estoril's casino in his first James Bond novel. Across the Tagus, the less fashionable southern shore could be reached only by ferry until the Ponte 25 de Abril was built in 1966. This swiftly opened up the long sandy beaches of the Costa da Caparica, the coast around the fishing town of Sesimbra and even the remote Tróia peninsula as popular summer resorts.

Torres Vedras

Carmões

Carnot

Encarnação

Turcifal

Sobral de
Monte Agraço

Ribamar

Santo Isidoro

Vila Franca do
Rosário

Aveiras de
Cima

N8

Sobreiro

Murgeira

Arranhó

A10

ERICEIRA 5

N116

A8

Milharado

PALÁCIO DE MAFRA 3

A21

Malveira

Bucelas

Alverca de
Ribatejo

LISBOA

A1

N247

N9

Cheleiros

Lousa

A9

São João das
Lampas

Pero Pinheiro

Póvoa de
Santa Iria

Azenhas do Mar

N117

Loures

São João
da Talha

Praia das Maças

Caneças

Sacavém

COLARES 4

SINTRA 1

A16

Odivelas

Portela
Airport ✈

A12

*Cabo da
Roca*

MONSERRATE 6

Belas

Serra de Sintra

**PALÁCIO NACIONAL
DE QUELUZ** 2

Malveira da Serra

A16

Alcabideche

LISBON

Guincho

A9

A5

Caxias

Almada

ESTORIL 7

Boca do Inferno

8

Oeiras

A2

CASCAIS

Carcavelos

Trafaria

Barreir

COSTA DA CAPARICA 10

Areeiro

Seixal

A33

N10

A2

Coi

Marco do Grilo

A t l a n t i c

O c e a n

*Lagoa de
Albufeira*

N379

Alfarim

Santana

11

SESIMBRA

Nossa Senhora
do Cabo

12

CABO ESPICHEL

0 kilometres   10

0 miles   10

N
↑

THE LISBON COAST

Must Sees

1. Sintra
2. Palácio Nacional de Queluz

Experience More

3. Palácio de Mafra
4. Colares
5. Ericeira
6. Monserrate
7. Estoril
8. Cascais
9. Alcochete
10. Costa da Caparica
11. Sesimbra
12. Cabo Espichel
13. Palmela
14. Serra da Arrábida
15. Península de Tróia
16. Setúbal
17. Alcácer do Sal

↑ Sintra's spectacular skyline, dominated by the Palácio Nacional

①

SINTRA

29 km (18 miles) NW of Lisbon 🚇🚌 Avenida Dr Miguel Bombarda; bus 434 runs from station to all the major sights 🛈 Praça da República 23; 219 231 157

Sintra's stunning setting on the north slopes of the granite Serra made it a favourite summer retreat for the kings of Portugal – resulting in the construction of a number of quirkily spectacular palaces. Today, the town (recognized as a UNESCO Cultural Landscape Site in 1995) draws thousands of visitors all through the year. Nevertheless, many quiet walks can be found in the beautiful surrounding wooded hills.

① 🖼️

Museu de História Natural de Sintra

🏠 Rua do Paço 20 📞 219 238 563 🕐 10am-6pm Tue-Fri, 12–6pm Sat & Sun 🚫 Mon and public hols

Located in the town's historic centre, Sintra's excellent natural history museum features a huge permanent collection of fossils and other ancient exhibits dating back several millennia. Housed in a striking 19th-century building, the museum also hosts regular temporary exhibitions relating to Portugal's natural history.

② 🖼️

Museu das Artes de Sintra

🏠 Avenida Helliodoro Salgado 📞 965 233 692 🕐 Apr-Sep: 10am-8pm Tue-Fri, 2–8pm Sat & Sun; Oct-Mar: 10am-6pm Tue-Fri, 12–6pm Sat & Sun 🚫 Public hols

This museum displays Portuguese and international artworks, with the permanent exhibition featuring the private collections of Emílio Paula Campos and Dórita Castel-Branco, and several landscapes of Sintra dating from the mid-18th century.

③ 🖼️🏍️🍴🛍️

Quinta da Regaleira

🏠 Rua Barbosa du Bocage 🚌 435 🕐 9:30am-6pm daily (to 8pm Apr-Sep) 🌐 regaleira.pt

Built between 1904 and 1910, this palace and its extensive gardens are a feast of historical and religious references, occult symbols and mystery. The brainchild of eccentric millionaire António Augusto Carvalho Monteiro, the grounds are riddled with secret passages and hidden tunnels. Sintra's local government reclaimed the site as a national monument in 1997 and opened it to the public shortly afterwards.

↑ Spiral Initiation Wells at the Quinta da Regaleira

④ Parque da Pena

Estra da Pena ◆Mar-late Oct: 9:30am-8pm daily; Nov-early Mar: 10am-6pm daily (last adm 1 hour before closing) ◆1 Jan, 25 Dec ◆parquesdesintra.pt

A huge park surrounds the Palácio Nacional da Pena, and hidden among the foliage are gazebos, follies and fountains, and a chalet built by Fernando II for his second wife, the Countess of Edla, in 1869. Cruz Alta, the highest point of the Serra at 529 m (1,740 ft), commands spectacular views of the Serra and surrounding plain. On a nearby crag is a statue known as "The Warrior", which supposedly symbolizes the king watching over his park and palace.

⑤ Castelo dos Mouros

Estrada da Pena ◆Mar-late Oct: 9:30am-8pm daily; Nov-early Mar: 10am-6pm daily (last adm 1 hour before closing) ◆1 Jan, 25 Dec ◆parquesdesintra.pt

Above the old town, the ramparts of the 10th-century Moorish castle conquered by Afonso Henriques in 1147 snake over the top of the Serra. On a fine day, there are great views from the castle walls over the old town to Palácio Nacional da Pena and along the coast. Hidden inside the walls is an ancient Moorish cistern, while the gateway's carved monogram ("DFII") is a reminder that Fernando II restored the castle in the 19th century.

STAY

Lawrence's
Spend the night at Lawrence's, Sintra's oldest hotel famously patronized by Lord Byron in the early 1800s. It's located in an 18th-century mansion, within which visitors can expect charmingly decorated rooms and an elegant restaurant.

Rua Consiglieri Pedroso 38, 2710-550 Sintra ◆lawrenceshotel.com

€€€

⑥ ⊛ ⊛

PALÁCIO NACIONAL DE SINTRA

⌂ Largo Rainha Dona Amélia ⏱ Mar-late Oct: 9:30am-7pm daily;
Nov-early Mar: 9:30am-6pm daily (last adm 30 mins before closing)
📅 1 Jan, 25 Dec 🌐 parquesdesintra.pt

One of the best-preserved royal palaces in Portugal, Sintra's National Palace has a fascinating mix of Moorish and Manueline architecture. Inside, the lavishly decorated, whimsically themed rooms are a delight to explore.

At the heart of the old town of Sintra (Sintra Vila), a pair of strange conical chimneys rise above the Royal Palace. The main part of the palace, including this central block with its plain Gothic façade, was built by João I in the late 14th century, on a site once occupied by the Moorish rulers. The Paço Real, as it is also known, soon became the favourite summer retreat for the court, and continued as a residence for Portuguese royalty until 1910. Additions to the building by Manuel I, in the early 16th century, echo the Moorish style. The palace stretches across a number of levels, in acquiescence to the mountain on which it sits.

The Sala dos Brasões, one of Europe's most impressive heraldry rooms

Did You Know?

Afonso VI was imprisoned by his brother, Pedro II, in the palace for nine years.

Sala das Galés (galleons)

Jardim da Preta, a walled garden

Quarto de Dom Sebastião, the bedroom of the young king

← The white walls and distinctive chimneys of the Palácio Nacional de Sintra

1 The domed ceiling of the Sala dos Brasões is decorated with stags holding the coats of arms (*brasões*) of 72 noble Portuguese families. The lower walls are lined with 18th-century Delft-like tiled panels.

2 The Ala Manuelina (Manuel's Wing) was built between 1497 and 1530 and the rooms are adorned with tiles from Seville.

3 The magnificent ceiling of the former banqueting hall is divided into octagonal panels decorated with swans (*cisnes*), each wearing an elegant golden collar.

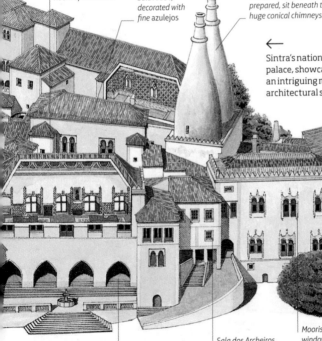

Sala das Sereias, or Room of the Sirens

Sala Árabe, decorated with fine azulejos

The kitchens, where royal banquets were once prepared, sit beneath the huge conical chimneys.

← Sintra's national palace, showcasing an intriguing meld of architectural styles

Entrance

Sala dos Archeiros, the entrance hall

Moorish-style windows on the Ala Manuelina

Timeline				
8th Century First palace established here by the Moors	**1147** Christian reconquest; Afonso Henriques takes over palace	**1495** Reign of Manuel I begins; major palace restoration and additions	**1755** Parts of palace damaged in great earthquake	**1910** Palace becomes a national monument

⑦ 🔧 🍴

PALÁCIO NACIONAL DA PENA

📍 Estrada da Pena, 5 km (3 miles) S of Sintra 🚌 434 from Avenida Dr Miguel Bombarda, Sintra 🕐 Mar-late Oct: 9:45am-7pm daily; Nov-early Mar: 10am-6pm daily 🚫 1 Jan, 25 Dec 🌐 parquesdesintra.pt

On the highest peaks of the Serra de Sintra stands the spectacular palace of Pena. Built in the 19th century for Queen Maria II's flamboyantly creative husband, Ferdinand Saxe-Coburg-Gotha, it comprises an eclectic medley of architectural styles.

The bright pink-and-yellow walls of the palace stand over the ruins of a Hieronymite monastery, founded here in the 15th century. Ferdinand appointed a German architect, Baron Von Eschwege, to build his dream summer palace, filled with international oddities and surrounded by a park. Construction started in 1840, and the extravagant project would ultimately last 45 years – the rest of the king's life. With the declaration of the Republic in 1910, the palace became a museum, preserved as it was when the royal family lived here.

Manuel II's bedroom, an oval-shaped room decorated with a stuccoed ceiling

Kitchen, where the dinner service still bears Ferdinand's coat of arms

① The brightly painted hilltop palace is a UNESCO World Heritage Site.

② Trompe l'oeil frescoes cover the walls and ceiling of the Arab Room, one of the loveliest in the palace.

③ The exterior is adorned with intricate architecture, heavily inspired by European Romanticism.

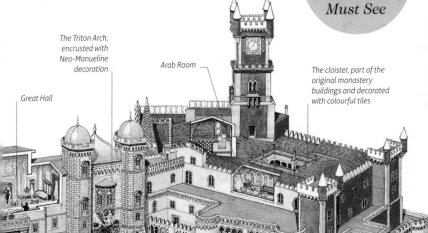

The Triton Arch, encrusted with Neo-Manueline decoration

Arab Room

The cloister, part of the original monastery buildings and decorated with colourful tiles

Great Hall

← The Romanticist Palácio Nacional da Pena, located in the hills of Sintra

Entrance

Entrance arch, a studded archway topped with crenellated turrets

FERDINAND: KING CONSORT

Born a German prince, Ferdinand was known in Portugal as Dom Fernando II, the "artist" king. Like his cousin Prince Albert, who married the English Queen Victoria, he loved art, nature and new inventions of the time. He was himself a watercolour painter. Ferdinand enthusiastically adopted his new country and devoted his life to patronizing the arts. In 1869, 16 years after the death of Maria II, Ferdinand married his mistress, the opera singer Countess Edla. His long-held dream of building the astonishing palace at Pena was finally completed in 1885, the year he died.

2 🏛 🖥 🍴

PALÁCIO NACIONAL DE QUELUZ

📍 Largo do Palácio, Queluz; 14 km (9 miles) NW of Lisbon 🚌 From Lisbon (Colégio Militar) 🚆 Queluz-Belas or Quelez-Massama ⏰ Mar-late Oct: 9am-7pm daily (last adm 1 hr before closing); Nov-early Mar: 9am-5:30pm daily (last adm 30 mins before closing) 🚫 1 Jan, 25 Dec 🌐 parquesdesintra.pt

Often referred to as Lisbon's Versailles, this palace is an excellent example of 18th-century Portuguese architecture. Initially intended as a summer residence, the royal family lived here permanently from 1794 until their departure for Brazil in 1807.

In 1747, Pedro, younger son of João V, commissioned Mateus Vicente to transform his 17th-century hunting lodge into a Rococo summer palace. The central section, including a music room and chapel, was built first, and after Pedro's marriage in 1760 to the future Maria I, the palace was again extended. The French architect Jean-Baptiste Robillion added the sumptuous Robillion Pavilion and gardens, cleared space for the throne room and redesigned the music room. During Maria's reign, the royal family kept a menagerie and went boating on the *azulejo*-lined canal.

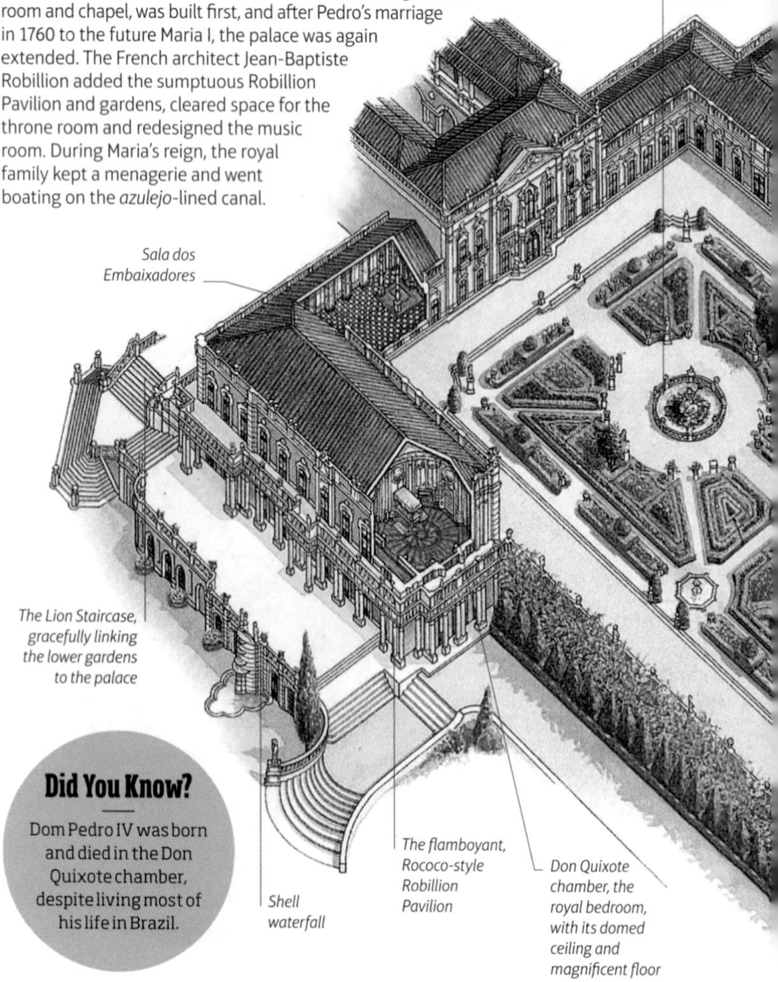

Neptune's Fountain

Sala dos Embaixadores

The Lion Staircase, gracefully linking the lower gardens to the palace

Did You Know?

Dom Pedro IV was born and died in the Don Quixote chamber, despite living most of his life in Brazil.

Shell waterfall

The flamboyant, Rococo-style Robillion Pavilion

Don Quixote chamber, the royal bedroom, with its domed ceiling and magnificent floor

1. The palace's ornate façade overlooks the spectacular Neptune's Fountain.

2. The formal gardens, adorned with statues, fountains and topiary, were often used for entertaining.

3. The Sala dos Embaixadores was a stately room built by Robillon and used for both diplomatic audiences and concerts.

1

2

3

The royal family's living rooms and bedrooms, which opened out onto the Malta Gardens

Chapel

Music room, where Maria I's orchestra performed operas and concerts

Entrance

Throne room

← The palace and its carefully arranged formal gardens

Malta Gardens

The Hanging Gardens, elaborately designed by Robillion and built over arches

MARIA I (1734–1816)

Maria, the eldest daughter of José I, lived at Queluz palace after her marriage to her uncle, Pedro. Serious and devout, Maria was a conscientious queen, but suffered increasingly from bouts of melancholia. When her son José died from smallpox in 1788, she went hopelessly mad. Visitors to Queluz were dismayed by her agonizing shrieks as she suffered visions and hallucinations. After the 1807 invasion, her younger son João took Maria to Brazil.

EXPERIENCE MORE

③  Palácio de Mafra

⌂ Terreiro de Dom João V, Mafra ▦ From Lisbon Ⓜ Campo Grande, then ⌂ Ericeira ⏰ 9:30am–5:30pm Wed–Mon (last adm 4:45pm) ⌂ 1 Jan, Easter, 1 May, 24 & 25 Dec Ⓦ palaciomafra.gov.pt

This massive Baroque palace and monastery were built during the reign of João V, and began with a vow by the young king to build a new monastery and basilica, supposedly in return for an heir. Work began in 1717 on a modest project but, as wealth began to pour into the royal coffers from Brazil, the king and his Italian-trained architect, Johann Friedrich Ludwig (1670–1752), made ever more extravagant plans. No expense was spared: the finished project housed 330 friars, a royal palace and one of the finest libraries in Europe, decorated with precious marble, exotic wood and countless works of art. The magnificent basilica was consecrated on the king's 41st birthday, 22 October 1730.

The palace was only popular with those members of the royal family who enjoyed hunting deer and wild boar. Most of the finest furniture

1717

Construction of the Palácio de Mafra began, a project so ambitious it almost bankrupted the state.

and art works were taken to Brazil when the royal family escaped the French invasion in 1807. The monastery was abandoned in 1834 following the dissolution of all religious orders, and the palace itself was abandoned in 1910.

The tour starts in the rooms of the monastery, through the pharmacy, with some alarming medical instruments, to the hospital, where patients could see and hear Mass in the adjoining chapel from their beds.

Upstairs, the sumptuous state rooms extend across the whole of the west façade, with the king's apartments at one end and the queen's apartments at the other. Midway, the long, imposing façade is relieved by the twin towers of the domed basilica. The church's interior is decorated in contrasting colours of marble and furnished with six early-19th-century organs. Mafra's greatest treasure, however, is its library, with its Rococo-style wooden bookcases and a collection of over 40,000 books in

gold-embossed leather bindings, including a prized first edition of *Os Lusíadas* (1572) by the Portuguese poet, Luís de Camões (1524–80).

④ Colares

▦ 𝒾 Cabo da Roca; 219 280 081

On the lower slopes of the Serra de Sintra, this lovely village faces the sea over a green valley. A leafy avenue winds its way up to the village. Small quantities of the famous Colares wine are still made. The hardy vines grow in sandy soil, with the roots set deep in clay;

→ Natural rock pool at the coastal town of Azenhas do Mar, near Colares

these were among the few vines in Europe to survive the disastrous phylloxera epidemic brought from America in the late 19th century. The insect ate the vines' roots but could not penetrate the dense sandy soil of the Atlantic coast. The Adega Regional de Colares on Alameda de Coronel Linhares de Lima offers wine tastings.

There are several popular beach resorts west of Colares. Just north of Praia das Maçãs is the picturesque village of Azenhas do Mar, clinging to the cliffs; to the south is the larger resort of Praia Grande.

5

Ericeira

🚌 ℹ️ **Rua Dr Eduardo Burnay 46; 261 863 122**

Ericeira is an old fishing village that keeps its traditions despite an ever-increasing influx of summer visitors who enjoy the bracing climate, clean,

←

The impressive Baroque façade of the Palácio de Mafra

sandy beaches and fresh seafood. In July and August, pavement cafés, restaurants and bars around the tree-lined Praça da República are buzzing late into the night. Alternative attractions include Santa Marta park and a history museum (closed until 2020).

The unspoilt old town, a maze of whitewashed houses and narrow, cobbled streets, is perched high above the ocean. From Largo das Ribas, at the top of a 30-m (100-ft) stone-faced cliff, there is a bird's-eye view over the busy fishing harbour below, where tractors haul the boats out of reach of the tide. In mid-August, the annual fishermen's festival is celebrated with a candlelit procession to the harbour at the foot of the cliffs for the blessing of the boats.

On 5 October 1910, Manuel II, the last king of Portugal, sailed into exile from Ericeira as the Republic was declared in Lisbon; a tiled panel in the fishermen's chapel of Santo António above the harbour records the event. The banished king settled in Twickenham, southwest London, where he died in 1932.

←

The Palace of Monserrate's beautifully wrought Romantic architecture, inside *(inset)* and out

6 ♿

Monserrate

🏠 Rua Barbosa du Bocage
🚉 To Sintra, then taxi or bus 435 🕐 Late Mar-late Oct: 9:30am-8pm daily (to 7pm for the palace); late Oct-late Mar: 10am-6pm daily (to 5pm for the palace)
🚫 1 Jan, 25 Dec
🌐 parquesdesintra.pt

The wild, romantic garden of this once magnificent estate is full of exotic trees and flowering shrubs. Among the subtropical foliage and valley of tree ferns are a small lake and a chapel, built as a ruin, tangled in the roots of a giant *Ficus* tree. Its history dates back to the Moors but it takes its name from a small 16th-century chapel dedicated to Our Lady of Montserrat in Catalonia, Spain. The gardens were landscaped in the late 1700s by a wealthy young Englishman, William Beckford. They were later immortalized by Lord Byron in *Childe Harold's Pilgrimage* (1812).

In 1856, the abandoned estate was bought by another Englishman, Sir Francis Cook, who built a fantastic Moorish-style palace (which has been restored) and transformed the gardens with a large lawn, camellias and subtropical trees from all over the world.

> 💬 INSIDER TIP
> **Fonte da Telha**
>
> Take the beach train from Caparica to the end of the line at Fonte da Telha. This is a popular family destination, but keep walking and you'll quickly find a patch of golden sands that you can have all to yourself.

7

Estoril

🚉🚌 🛈 Largo de Camões, Cascais; 912 034 214

The lovely resort town of Estoril is a tourist and business resort, and a place for comfortable retirement. What separates Estoril from Cascais, besides a pleasant beach promenade of 3 km (2 miles) and a mansion-covered ridge known as Monte Estoril, is its sense of place. The heart of Estoril is immediately accessible from the train station. On one side of the tracks is the riviera-like, but relaxed beach; on the other a palm-lined park flanked by grand buildings, stretching up past fountains to a casino. Dwarfing the casino is the Estoril Congress Centre, a vast multipurpose edifice that speaks confidently of Estoril's contemporary role.

→

Bathers enjoying the clear blue waters and sandy beach at Cascais

8

Cascais

🚌🚆 ℹ️ Largo de Camões; 912 034 214

A holiday resort for well over a century, Cascais possesses a certain illustriousness that younger resorts lack. Its history is visible in its villas, summer residences of wealthy Lisboetas who followed King Luís I's lead during the late 19th century.

Cascais today is a favoured suburb of Lisbon, a place of seaside apartments and pine-studded plots by golf courses. But the beautiful coastline beyond the town has been left largely undeveloped.

Housed in a castle-like villa, the **Museu Condes de Castro Guimarães** is the best place to get a taste of Cascais's history.

The **Casa das Histórias Paula Rego** is dedicated to the work of the painter, illustrator and printmaker.

Museu Condes de Castro Guimarães

◈ 📍 Avenida Rei Humberto de Itália 📞 214 815 304 🕙 10am–1pm, 2–5pm Tue–Sun

Casa das Histórias Paula Rego

◈ 📍 Avenida da República 300 🕙 10am–6pm Tue–Sun (Apr–Oct: to 7pm) 🌐 casadas historiaspaularego.com

9

Alcochete

🚌 ℹ️ Largo da Misericórdia; 212 348 655

This delightful old town overlooks the Tagus estuary from the southern shore. Salt has long been one of the main industries here, and saltpans can still be seen north and south of the town, while in the town centre a large statue of a muscular salt worker has the inscription: "Do Sal a Revolta e a Esperança" (From Salt to Rebellion and Hope).

The Reserva Natural do Estuário do Tejo covers a vast area of estuary water, salt marshes and small islands around Alcochete, and is a very important breeding ground for water birds.

10

Costa da Caparica

🚌 To Cacilhas or Trafaria then bus 🚆 To Pragal then bus ℹ️ Frente Urbana de Praias; 212 900 071

Long beaches backed by sand dunes make this a popular holiday resort for Lisboetas, who come to swim, sunbathe and enjoy the beach cafés and seafood restaurants. A railway with open carriages runs for 10 km (6 miles) along the coast in summer. The first beaches reached from the town are popular with families with children, while the furthest beaches suit those seeking quiet isolation.

EAT

O Pescador

This nautical-themed eatery is lined with wooden tables and fishing paraphernalia. Diners can sit on the pleasant outdoor terrace and enjoy the menu's emphasis on fresh fish.

📍 Rua das Flores 10b, Cascais 🕙 Wed L 🌐 restaurante pescador.com

€€€

Saudade

An appealing café and art gallery near the train station that serves coffees, cakes, sandwiches and *petiscos* (Portuguese tapas).

📍 Avenida Dr Miguel Bombarda 6, Sintra 📞 212 428 804

€€€

A palm-lined inlet and the Santa Marta lighthouse in Cascais

⑪ Sesimbra

🚌 ℹ️ Rua da Fortaleza de Santiago; 212 288 540

Protected from north winds by the slopes of the Serra da Arrábida, this busy fishing village has become a popular holiday resort. The old town is a maze of steep narrow streets, with the Santiago Fort (now a customs post) in the centre overlooking the sea. From the terrace there are views of the town, the Atlantic and the wide sandy beach that stretches out on either side. Sesimbra is fast developing as a resort, with plentiful pavement cafés and bars that are always busy on sunny days.

The fishing fleet is moored in the Porto do Abrigo to the west of the main town. The harbour is reached by taking Avenida dos Náufragos, a sweeping promenade that follows the beach out of town. When the fishing boats return from a day at sea, a colourful, noisy fish auction takes place on the quayside. The day's catch can be tasted in the town's excellent fish restaurants along the shore.

High above the town is the Moorish castle, greatly restored in the 18th century when a church and small flower-filled cemetery were added inside the walls. There are wonderful views from the ramparts, especially at sunset.

⑫ Cabo Espichel

🚌 From Sesimbra

Sheer cliffs drop straight into the sea on this windswept promontory. The Romans named it Promontorium Barbaricum, alluding to its dangerous location, and a lighthouse warns sailors of the treacherous rocks below. Stunning views of the ocean and the coast can be enjoyed from this bleak outcrop of land but beware of the strong gusts of wind on the cliff edge.

In this desolate setting is the impressive Santuário de Nossa Senhora do Cabo, a late-17th-century church with its back to the sea. On either side of the church, a long line of pilgrims' lodgings, facing inwards, form an open courtyard. Baroque paintings, *ex votos* and a frescoed ceiling decorate the church's interior. Nearby, a domed chapel has tiled blue-and-white *azulejo* panels depicting fishing scenes. The site became a popular place of pilgrimage in the 13th century when a local man had a vision of the Madonna rising from the sea on a mule. Legend has it that the mule tracks can be seen embedded in the rock.

⑬ Palmela

🏰 🚌 ℹ️ Castelo de Palmela; 212 332 122

The formidable castle at Palmela stands over the small hill town, high on a north-eastern spur of the wooded Serra da Arrábida. Its strategic position dominates the plain for miles around, especially when floodlit at night. Heavily defended by the Moors, it was finally conquered in the 12th century and given by Sancho I to the Knights of the Order of Santiago. In 1423, João I transformed the castle into a monastery for the Order. It has since been restored and converted into a splendid

↓ Brightly painted fishing boats moored in the harbour at Sesimbra

The castle at Palmela
with views over the
Serra da Arrábida

pousada, with a restaurant in the monks' refectory and a swimming pool for residents, hidden inside the castle walls.

From the castle terraces and the top of the 14th-century keep, there are fantastic views over the Serra da Arrábida to the south, and on a clear day across the Tagus to Lisbon. In the town square below, the church of São Pedro contains 18th-century tiles of scenes from the life of St Peter.

The annual wine festival, the Festa das Vindimas, is held on the first weekend of September in front of the 17th-century Paços do Concelho (town hall). Traditionally dressed villagers press the wine barefoot and on the final day of celebrations there is a spectacular firework display from the castle walls.

14

Serra da Arrábida

🚌From Setúbal 🏛Parque Natural da Arrábida, Praça da República, Setúbal; 265 541 140

The Serra da Arrábida Natural Park covers the range of limestone mountains that stretches east–west along the coast between Sesimbra and Setúbal. It was established to protect the wild, beautiful landscape and rich variety of birds and wildlife, including wildcats and badgers.

The sheltered, south-facing slopes are thickly covered with aromatic and evergreen shrubs and trees, such as pine and cypress, more typical of the Mediterranean. Vineyards also thrive on the sheltered slopes and the town of Vila Nogueira de Azeitão is particularly known for its wine, Moscatel de Setúbal.

The Estrada de Escarpa (the N379-1) snakes across the top of the ridge and affords astounding views. A narrow road winds down to Portinho da Arrábida, a sheltered cove with a beach of fine white sand and crystal clear sea, popular with underwater fishermen. The sandy beaches of Galapos and Figueirinha are a little further east along the coast road towards Setúbal. Just east of Sesimbra, the Serra da Arrábida drops to the sea in the sheer 380-m (1,250-ft) cliffs of Risco, the highest in mainland Portugal.

> **From the castle terraces and the top of the 14th-century keep, there are fantastic views over the Serra da Arrábida to the south, and on a clear day across the Tagus to Lisbon.**

EAT

O Barbas Catedral

This renowned restaurant, which overlooks the breakers of Caparica beach, is usually packed at weekends thanks to its delicious seafood dishes.

🏠 Apoio de Praia 13, Caparica
📞 212 900 163

€€€

O Galeão

Expect sparkling sea views from the terrace, great salads and fresh fish at this restaurant above the water.

🏠 Portinho da Arrábida
📞 212 180 533

€€€

Ribamar

This upmarket restaurant is right on the seafront, and has been serving tasty seafood dishes for over 60 years.

🏠 Avenida dos Náufragos 29, Sesimbra
🌐 ribamar.pt

€€€

---

⑮

Península de Tróia

🚍🚢 Tróia 🛈 Tróia Resort; 265 499 400
🕐 Cetóbriga: Mar-Oct: 10am-1pm, 2:30-6pm Wed-Sun (to 6:30pm Jun-Aug)

Holiday apartments dominate the tip of the Tróia Peninsula, easily accessible from Setúbal by ferry. The Atlantic coast, stretching south for 18 km (11 miles) of untouched sandy beaches, is now the haunt of sun-seekers in the summer.

Near Tróia, in the sheltered lagoon, the Roman town of Cetóbriga was the site of a thriving fish-salting business; the stone tanks and ruined buildings are open to visit.

Further on, Carrasqueira is an old fishing community where you can still see traditional reed houses, with walls and roofs made from thatch.

---

⑯

Setúbal

🚍🚢🚆 🛈 Casa da Baía, Ave Luísa Todi 468; 265 545 010

An important industrial town and the third-largest port in Portugal (after Lisbon and Porto), Setúbal makes a good base from which to explore the area. To the south of the central gardens and fountains are the fishing harbour, marina and

Did You Know?

One of Setúbal's most famous sons is football manager José Mourinho, born here in 1963.

ferry port, and a lively covered market. North of the gardens is the old town, with attractive pedestrian streets and squares full of cafés.

The 16th-century cathedral, dedicated to Santa Maria da Graça, has glorious 18th-century tiled panels, and gilded altar decoration. Street names commemorate two famous Setúbal residents: Manuel Barbosa du Bocage (1765–1805), whose satirical poetry landed him in prison, and Luísa Todi (1753–1833), a celebrated opera singer.

In Roman times, fish-salting was the most important industry here. Rectangular stone tanks used for this process can still be seen on Travessa Frei Gaspar.

To the north of the old town, the striking Igreja de Jesus (currently closed for restoration) is one of Setúbal's treasures. Designed by the architect Diogo Boitac in 1494, the lofty interior is adorned with twisted columns, of pinkish Arrábida limestone

← Jetty with fishing boats moored on the mud flats at Carrasqueira

and rope-like stone ribs, recognized as the first examples of the distinctive Manueline style.

On Rua do Balneário, in the old monastic quarters, a museum houses 14 remarkable paintings of the life of Christ. The works are attributed to followers of the Renaissance painter Jorge Afonso (1520–30).

The **Museu de Arquelogia e Etnografia** displays a wealth of finds from digs around Setúbal, including Bronze Age pots and Roman coins. The ethnography display shows local arts, crafts and industries, including the processing of salt and cork over the centuries.

The star-shaped **Castelo de São Filipe** was built in 1595 by Philip II of Spain during the period of Spanish rule to keep a wary eye on pirates, English invaders and the local population. It now houses a boutique hotel, but the battlements and ramparts are open to the public and offer marvellous views over the city and the Sado estuary.

Setúbal is an ideal starting point for a tour by car of the unspoilt Reserva Natural do Estuário do Sado, a vast stretch of mud flats, shallow lagoons and salt marshes, which has been explored and inhabited since 3500 BC.

Museu de Arquelogia e Etnografia

🏠 Avenida Luísa Todi 162
🕙 9am–12:30pm, 2–5:30pm Tue–Sat 🚫 Public hols
🌐 maeds.amrs.pt

Castelo de São Filipe

🎫 🏠 Estrada de São Felipe
🕙 10am–noon, 1–6pm Tue–Sun (to midnight Fri & Sat)

> **ANIMALS OF THE SADO ESTUARY**
>
> A protected nature reserve, the Sado estuary is an area of salt marsh home to nesting storks and flamingos, and the only place along the Portuguese coast where you can see wild bottlenose dolphins. Many water birds, including avocets and pratincoles, are found close to the areas of open water and dried-out lagoons of the estuary, where reedbeds provide shelter.

17

Alcácer do Sal

🏠🚌 𝒊 Largo Luís de Camões; 911 794 685

Bypassed by the main road, the ancient town of Alcácer do Sal (al-kasr from the Arabic for castle, and do sal from its trade in salt) sits peacefully on the north bank of the Sado river. The imposing castle was a hillfort as early as the 6th century BC. The Phoenicians made an inland trading port here, and the castle later became a Roman stronghold. Rebuilt by the Moors, it was conquered by Afonso II in 1217. The buildings have now taken on a new life as a pousada, with views over the rooftops. Also notable here is the **Cripta Arqueológica do Castelo**, an archaeological museum holding locally excavated items. The collections include artifacts from the Iron Age, as well as from the Roman, Moorish and medieval periods.

There are pleasant cafés along the riverside promenade and several historic churches.

Cripta Arqueológica do Castelo

♿ 🏠 Castelo de Alcácer do Sal 📞 265 612 058
🕙 9am–12:30pm, 2–5:30pm Tue–Sat 🚫 Public hols

Tiled chapel in Castelo de São Filipe, Setúbal ↑

A DRIVING TOUR
SERRA DE SINTRA

Length 36 km (22 miles) **Stopping-off points** Cabo da Roca; Colares **Terrain** Mountainous in places, with steep, narrow roads

This round trip from Sintra follows a dramatic route over the top of the wooded Serra. The first part is a challenging drive with hazardous hairpin bends on steep, narrow roads that are at times poorly surfaced. It passes through dense forest and a surreal landscape of giant moss-covered boulders, with breathtaking views over the Atlantic coast, the Tagus estuary and beyond. After dropping down to the rugged, windswept coast, the route returns to small country roads, passing through hill villages and large estates on the cool, green northern slopes of the Serra de Sintra.

The village of **Colares** *rests on the lower slopes of the wooded Serra, surrounded by gardens and vineyards (p160). There are several delightful bars and restaurants here too.*

Cabo da Roca makes a good stopping-off point, offering spectacular ocean views, along with a café and souvenir shop.

A lighthouse at the top of an impressive cliff, 140 m (459 ft) high, marks the most westerly point of the European mainland.

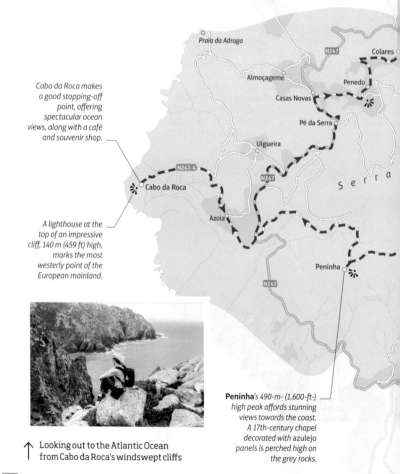

Praia da Adraga

Colares

Almoçageme

Penedo

Casas Novas

Pé da Serra

Ulgueira

Cabo da Roca

Azoia

Serra

Peninha

Peninha's 490-m- (1,600-ft-) high peak affords stunning views towards the coast. A 17th-century chapel decorated with azulejo panels is perched high on the grey rocks.

↑ Looking out to the Atlantic Ocean from Cabo da Roca's windswept cliffs

Visitors climbing
the 10th-century
Castelo dos Mouros

Serra de
Sintra Tour

Locator Map
For more detail see p150

End this drive at
Seteais. *Now a luxury
hotel and restaurant,
this elegant palace was
built in the 18th century
for the Dutch Consul,
Daniel Gildemeester.*

The cool forest park and
elaborate 19th-century palace of
Monserrate *epitomize the
romanticism of Sintra (p162).*

From the centre
of **Sintra**'s old town
*(p152), the road winds
steeply upwards past
magnificent quintas
(country estates) hidden
among the trees.*

Ribeira de Colares   N247

N375   Galamares

N247

Sintra

Seteais

N375
FINISH

Castelo dos
Mouros

Montserrate

*Parque
da Pena*

Convento dos Capuchos

S i n t r a

△
Monte Rodel
392 m

START

Palácio Nacional da Pena

N9

△
Monge
490 m

N247-3   N247-3

Rio da Mula

SINTRA

△
Pedra Branca
359 m

Albufeira do
Rio da Mula

△
Pedra Amarela
408 m

The spectacular
**Palácio Nacional de
Pena** *perches on the
highest peaks of the
Serra Sintra (p156).*

*Two huge boulders guard the entrance
to this remote Franciscan monastery.
The* **Convento dos Capuchos** *was
founded in 1560 and where friars lived
in tiny rock-hewn cells lined with cork.*

Begin this drive
at the **Parque
da Pena.** *This
huge, exotic park
can be explored
on foot (p153).*

0 kilometres   1

0 miles   1

N
↑

NEED TO KNOW

BEFORE
YOU GO

Forward planning is essential for any successful trip. Prepare yourself for any eventuality by brushing up on the following points before you set off.

CURRENCY
Euro (EUR)

AVERAGE DAILY SPEND

SAVE	SPEND	SPLURGE
€35	€70	€150+

BOTTLED WATER	COFFEE	BEER	DINNER FOR TWO
€0.80	€1	€3	€45

ESSENTIAL PHRASES

Hello	Olá
Thank you	Obrigado/Obrigada
Please	Por favor
Goodbye	Adeus
Do you speak English	Fala inglês?
I don't understand	Não compreendo

ELECTRICITY SUPPLY

Power sockets are type F, fitting a two-prong plug. Standard voltage is 220–240v.

Passports and Visas

EU nationals may visit for an unlimited period, registering with local authorities after 3 months. Citizens of the US, Canada, Australia and New Zealand can reside without a visa for up to 90 days. For those arriving from other countries, check with your local Portuguese embassy or on the **Camara Municipal website**.
Camara Municipal
w cm-lisboa.pt/en

Travel Safety Advice

Visitors can get up-to-date travel safety inform-ation from the **UK Foreign and Commonwealth Office**, the **US State Department** and the **Australian Department of Foreign Affairs and Trade**.
AUS
w smartraveller.gov.au
UK
w gov.uk/foreign-travel-advice
US
w travel.state.gov

Customs Information

An individual is permitted to carry the following within the EU for personal use:
Tobacco products 800 cigarettes, 400 cigarillos, 200 cigars or 1 kg of smoking tobacco.
Alcohol 10 litres of alcoholic beverages above 22% strength, 20 litres of alcoholic beverages below 22% strength, 90 litres of wine (60 litres of which can be sparkling wine) and 110 litres of beer.
Cash If you plan to enter or leave the EU with €10,000 or more in cash (or the equivalent in other currencies) you must declare it to the customs authorities.

Language

English is widely spoken in Portugal's cities, but the Portuguese are proud of their language and appreciate visitors' efforts to communicate. While written Portuguese is similar to Spanish,

the idiosyncratic pronunciation of spoken Portuguese can demand several attempts to correctly enunciate even simple phrases. Attempting to communicate solely in Spanish may cause offence.

Insurance

It is wise to take out an insurance policy covering theft, loss of belongings, medical problems, cancellations and delays. EU citizens are eligible for free emergency medical care in Portugal provided they have a valid **EHIC** (European Health Insurance Card).
EHIC.
☒ gov.uk/european-health-insurance-card

Vaccinations

No inoculations are necessary for Portugal.

Booking Accommodation

Lisbon offers a variety of accommodation, ranging from boutique hotels to campsites, budget hostels to private apartment rentals. A list of accommodation can be found on the **Visit Portugal** website.

During the summer months, lodgings are snapped up fast and prices become inflated, so book in advance. Lisbon is a popular short city-break destination, and it can also be difficult to find a last-minute weekend booking during the low season (Dec–Mar).

Visitors to Lisbon are required to pay a €1/night city tourism tax for stays up to 7 days, which is payable on top of your bill. Children below the age of 13 are exempt. Hotels are required by law to share details of foreign visitors with the local authorities.
Visit Portugal
☒ visitportugal.com

Money

Most establishments accept major credit, debit and prepaid currency cards. Contactless payments are gradually becoming more common in Lisbon, but it's always a good idea to carry cash for smaller items like coffee and *pastéis de nata*, or when visiting markets. ATMs are widely available across the city.

Travellers with Specific Needs

Lisbon's hills can prove a challenge to navigate for wheelchair-users and those with prams. Facilities in Lisbon have improved over recent years, with wheelchairs, adapted toilets, and reserved car parking available at the airports and main stations. Ramps and lifts are installed in many public places and some buses (marked with a blue-and-white logo at the front) accommodate wheelchair-users.

Tour companies, such as **Tourism For All,** offer specialist holiday packages, while **Accessible Portugal** gives comprehensive advice on travelling with limited mobility.
Accessible Portugal
☒ accessibleportugal.com
Tourism For All
☒ tourism-for-all.com

Closures

Lunchtime Some museums and public buildings may close from noon until 2pm.

Monday State-run museums, public buildings and monuments are closed all day.

Sunday Churches and cathedrals are closed to tourists during Mass. Some public transport runs less frequently.

Public holidays Most museums, public buildings and many shops close early or for the day.

PUBLIC HOLIDAYS	
1 Jan	New Year's Day
Mar/Apr	Good Friday
Mar/Apr	Easter Sunday
25 Apr	Freedom Day
1 May	Labour Day
10 Jun	Portugal Day
13 Jun	Feast of St Anthony
20 Jun	Corpus Christi
15 Aug	Assumption Day
5 Oct	Republic Day
1 Nov	All Saint's Day
1 Dec	Restoration of Independence
8 Dec	Immaculate Conception Day
25 Dec	Christmas Day

GETTING AROUND

Whether exploring Lisbon by foot or public transport, here is everything you need to know to navigate the city like a pro.

AT A GLANCE

PUBLIC TRANSPORT COSTS

METRO

€1.45

1 hour
transfers included

BUS

€1.80

single journey
on bus

TRAM

€2.85

single journey
on tram

SPEED LIMIT

MOTORWAY

120
km/h
(75m/h)

DUAL CARRIAGEWAY

100
km/h
(60m/h)

SECONDARY ROAD

90
km/h
(55m/h)

URBAN AREAS

50
km/h
(30m/h)

Arriving by Air

Lisbon Humberto Delgado Airport is served by local and international flights and has excellent transport links to the city centre. For journey times and ticket pricing for transport between the airport and the city centre, see the table opposite.
Lisbon Humberto Delgado Airport
W ana.pt

Train Travel

International Train Travel
There are two main routes into Portugal by train. The famous Sud Express train, which departs daily at 6:45pm from Irun on the French-Spanish border, can be reached from Austerlitz station in Paris. Travelling from London to Lisbon, using the **Eurostar** to reach Paris, and then the Sud Express to Lisbon, takes approximately 30 hours. Alternatively, the overnight train from Madrid takes 10 hours. Both routes are operated by the Spanish state-run service **Renfe.** You can purchase tickets online or at Lisbon's international train stations. It is sensible to book ahead in peak season (Jul–Aug).
Eurostar
W eurostar.com
Renfe
W renfe.com

Regional Trains
CP (Comboios de Portugal) is the country's national rail operator. Most parts of Portugal are served by rail, although the more remote lines have sadly been made obsolete by new road links. Lisbon has four main train stations: Rossio, Cais do Sodré, Santa Apolónia and Oriente. Rossio and Cais do Sodré cover local journeys with lines to Sintra and Cascais, respectively. Santa Apolónia and Oriente provide links to international destinations and those across Portugal, like Porto and Coimbra.

All trains should be pre-booked either online or at the station, except for journeys on urban rail networks (urbanas), such as the Sintra and Cascais lines. A conductor will validate tickets

GETTING TO AND FROM THE AIRPORT

Airport	Transport	Price	Journey time
Humberto Delgado Airport	Metro	€1.45	25 mins
	Bus (Aerobus)	€3.60	35 mins
	Taxi	€20	30 mins

on-board and will often ask for ID. Tickets for *urbanas* can be bought at the station prior to departure and should be validated at the ticket machines on the platform before boarding.
CP
w cp.pt

Public Transport

State-owned **Carris** is Lisbon's main public transport authority and is responsible for buses, trams and elevators. The metro is run separately, also by the state. Timetables, ticket information, maps and more can be found online, on the Carris app and inside some metro stations.
Carris
w carris.pt

Tickets
Single-trip paper tickets for buses, trams and funiculars can be bought upon boarding. Multi-trip paper tickets have been replaced with electronic passes, such as the tourist-friendly **Viva Viagem** smart card. This "Zapping" card costs €0.50 and each traveller must have their own. They can be purchased at vending machines and ticket offices in metro stations across the city, including Cais do Sodré and Marquês de Pombal, and some railway stations, shops and newsagents.

Buying a pre-paid Viva Viagem is the most practical option for visitors, as you can top up your card's balance whenever necessary, travelling across the Carris and metro networks at a lower price. You can also load Viva Viagem cards with a 24-hour pass, which allows unlimited travel with Carris and on the metro for €6.30. Passes that include the Tagus ferries (€9.35) or Sintra and Cascais train lines (€10.40) are also available. Note that the balance remaining on the card cannot be refunded.
Viva Viagem
w portalviva.pt

Metro
The fastest and cheapest way to get around town is by the **Metropolitano de Lisboa**. Metro stations are signposted with a red M, and the service operates from 6:30am to 1am every day. There are currently over 50 metro stations operating on four lines. These lines link the metro to major bus, train and ferry services, and provide transport from Lisbon's suburbs to the city centre.

Although the metro can be very busy during rush hour, there are frequent trains. The system is safe to travel on by night, since police regularly patrol the stations and trains.

All stations have automatic gates at the entrance to the platform and a valid ticket must be passed over the electronic scanner when entering and leaving the station.
Metropolitano de Lisboa
w metrolisboa.pt

Trams and Funiculars
Trams are a pleasant ways of sightseeing in Lisbon but they only operate in limited areas of the city, along the river to Belém and around the hillier parts of Lisbon. At €2.85 for a single trip without a Viva Viagem card, they can be a costly choice. The charming, pre-World War I models still run alongside new trams with sleek interiors. Perhaps the most popular route is tram 28, which passes by Alfama and Mouraria as it circumvents Castelo de São Jorge, before taking a scenic route across the city to the more grandiose districts of São Bento and Estrela.

Three historic funiculars (Gloria, Bica and Lavra) carry weary Lisboetas up several of the city's steepest hills, and are classed as national monuments. Similarly, the Elevador de Santa Justa is a useful and enjoyable tourist experience, but queues can be long.

Purchase a Viva Viagem card to minimize the cost of trams, funiculars and the Elevador de Santa Justa.

Buses

The bus network is Lisbon's most extensive public transport system, and buses go just about everywhere. They are usually yellow and are a bright feature around the city's streets, generally running from 5:30am to 1am in the inner city. A small number of night services continue outside these hours.

The bus timetable suffers from Lisbon's traffic problems, which means that you sometimes have to wait a long time to board a very crowded bus. Bus stops are indicated by a sign marked Paragem and display the routes that serve them, along with timetables. Many stops and buses now also display real-time schedule information.

Long-Distance Bus Travel

Sete Rios is Lisbon's main bus station and there are several private companies operating coach services. **Rede Expressos** covers most of Portugal, linking Braga, Porto, Lisbon and Faro. As a general rule, you can no longer buy tickets on-board for long distance trips. There are discounts for booking early, either online or in bus stations at the relevant company's kiosk.

Tickets for shorter trips, however, must be bought at the station or from the driver. **TST** serves destinations south of the Tagus. Buses leave from Praça de Espanha for destinations such as Costa da Caparica (1 hr) and Sesimbra (1 hr 45 mins). **EVA** covers the Algarve particularly well and is based at the Sete Rios bus terminal.

EVA
ⓦ eva-bus.com

Rede Expressos
ⓦ rede-expressos.pt/en/

TST
ⓦ tsuldotejo.pt

Boats and Ferries

The frequent commuter ferries over the Tagus river, which depart roughly every 15 minutes, make for a pleasant excursion to the port suburb of Cacilhas. Most ferry services on the Tagus are run by **Transtejo** and depart regularly from Cais do Sodré, Terreiro do Paço and Belém to several destinations south of the river. Ticket prices range from €0.50 with a Viva Viagem pass, to €2.40 for a return ferry trip. Trips generally last 15–25 minutes and are worth making purely for the fabulous views of Lisbon.

Transtejo
ⓦ transtejo.pt

Trips and Tours

There are two main hop-on hop-off tour bus operators in Lisbon although, due to the inner city's hilly nature, bus routes mostly follow the city's flatter outskirts, past sights such as the Torre de Belém, Basilica da Estrela and Parque Eduardo VII.

Trips on the red **City Sightseeing** buses cost around €22, with a choice of two routes through the east or west of the city. For a similar price, state-run **Carristur**'s yellow bus routes include a tour along the Tagus. Tickets for both companies are valid for 24 hours and can be purchased online or on-board.

Tuk-tuks, which are well suited to navigating the inner city and provide a more personalized, often exciting (or nerve-wracking) experience, have become popular in recent years. **Eco Tuk Tuk Lisbon** provides tours from around €70 for 1 hour. Alternatively you can haggle with the drivers lining the streets next to Sé Cathedral.

There is a large choice of tour operators offering trips of varying lengths to other cities in Portugal. Day trips from Lisbon include destinations like Sintra, Cabo da Roca and Cascais, or Arrábida's rugged coastline. Tours can be booked directly with the operator, through a travel agent and at some hotels.

Carristur
ⓦ carris.pt/en/carristur/

City Sightseeing
ⓦ city-sightseeing.com

Eco Tuk Tuk Lisbon
ⓦ ecotuktours.com

Taxis

Taxis in Lisbon are relatively inexpensive compared to the rest of Europe and can work out cheaper than public transport for large groups. Most drivers only accept cash and can be hailed in the street and at taxi ranks.

A green light indicates that the taxi is available and two green lights mean a higher rate. The normal starting rate for a taxi is €3.25 during the day and €3.90 at night. Ensure that the meter is on, suggest agreeing on a price for longer routes and always check the extra cost for luggage before setting off. Two of the largest firms are **Autocoope** and **Radio Taxis**, but taxi apps such as Uber also operate in Lisbon.

Autocoope
ⓦ autocoope.pai.pt

Radio Taxis
ⓦ taxislisboa.com

Driving

Driving around Lisbon can be a daunting experience, thanks to a complex street plan, traffic jams and scarce parking.

Driving to Lisbon

Though Portuguese roads are rightly renowned as accident-prone, in 2015 the World Economic

Forum pronounced the road network itself to be the best in Europe. There are seven roads into Lisbon. Those arriving from the south can cross to central Lisbon via the Ponte 25 de Abril or the newer Ponte Vasco de Gama. From the north, the A1 (E1) motorway brings you to Lisbon's north-eastern outskirts. Those arriving from Cascais and the Lisbon Coast enter via the tolled A5 motorway or the coastal N6 road.

Most of the main motorways in Portugal are toll roads, paid electronically. The easiest system to use is **EasyToll**, which matches your credit card to your licence plate and automatically deducts the necessary funds. Payments and details can be managed on their website.

If you bring your own foreign-registered car, you must carry a valid driver's licence, proof of ownership, insurance and address, as well as an up-to-date MOT certificate. After 183 days, the car must either be registered in Portugal or taken to another country.

EasyToll
W portugaltolls.com

Driving in Lisbon

City centre streets are narrow, difficult to navigate and often congested, and on-street parking is scant, so driving in Lisbon is not recommended. A vast network of ring roads traces the outskirts, although a missed or wrong exit can result in a severe detour.

The city offers relatively few on-street parking spaces, but there are many underground car parks, marked by signs with a white P on a blue background. **The European Car Parking Guide** lists car parks around Lisbon.

If your car is towed or clamped, contact **EMEL** based in Sete Rios. You will have to pay a fee of up to €300 to retrieve it, as well as pay for the parking violation.

EMEL
W emel.pt
The European Car Parking Guide
W car-parking.eu/portugal/lisbon/

Car Rental

Most major car hire companies have offices at the airport. To rent a car in Portugal you must be over 18 and have held a valid driver's licence for at least one year, although those under 25 may need to pay a surcharge.

Prices rise considerably in peak season (Jul–Aug) and some companies offer special off-peak (Dec–Mar) and weekend deals.

As Lisbon's streets are narrow and Portuguese drivers are infamously erratic, it is sensible to arrange third-party insurance beforehand or take the pricier "no excess" insurance deals offered upon pick-up. Most car hire companies give the option to pay all road toll fees upon the vehicle's return.

Rules of the Road

Drive on the right and use the left lane only for passing. Seat belts are required for all passengers and heavy fines are incurred for using a mobile phone while driving. Drivers are required to stop at pedestrian crossings. The blood-alcohol concentration (BAC) limit is 0.5mg/ml and is very strictly enforced. If you are drinking alcohol, use public transport or a taxi.

Always carry your passport, licence and insurance details. In the event of an accident or breakdown, the driver and passengers must don a fluorescent yellow safety vest and erect a collapsible warning triangle 50m behind the vehicle. Both of these items must be stored in the trunk at all times. Driver's licences issued by any EU member state are valid throughout the EU, including Portugal. If visiting from outside the EU, you may need to apply for an International Driving Permit (IDP). The local motoring association, the **ACP** (Automóvel Club de Portugal), has a reciprocal breakdown service with most other international motoring organizations. To qualify, drivers must take out European cover with their own organization. Should you be involved in a road accident, the emergency services number is 112. If you have simply broken down, call the ACP (808 502 502) or, if driving a hired car, check the instructions supplied by your chosen company.

ACP
W acp.pt

Cycle and Scooter Hire

Lisbon's hilly terrain does not make for easy cycling, but cycle paths do exist along the Tagus and in flatter areas. The vast Monsanto Forest Park can provide quieter roads and respite from the sun, while there are several popular cycle routes south of the river. A growing number of companies, including **Lisbon Bike Rentals**, now offer electric bikes.

Scooters and motorcycles are a more popular choice, particularly for those looking to explore the Lisbon Coast. Most companies require a deposit and ask that you leave your passport at the rental shop. You must have a driver's licence valid for your desired bike category. Note that 50cc vehicles are forbidden on motorways, which includes the Ponte 25 de Abril and Ponte Vasco de Gama. All riders must wear helmets by law, which can be rented from most hire shops. **LX Rent** is reliable and conveniently located where Alfama meets the Tagus, with scooters from €36/day.

Lisbon Bike Rentals
W lisbonbikerentals.com
LX Rent
W lxrent.pt

PRACTICAL
INFORMATION

A little local know-how goes a long way in Lisbon. Here is all the essential advice and information you will need during your stay.

AT A GLANCE

EMERGENCY NUMBERS

GENERAL EMERGENCY	AMBULANCE
112	**118**

FIRE SERVICE	POLICE
115	**112**

TIME ZONE
CET/CEST
Central European
Summer time (CEST)
runs end Mar-end Oct

TAP WATER
Unless stated
otherwise, tap
water in Lisbon is
safe to drink.

TIPPING

Waiter	10%
Hotel Porter	€1-2
Housekeeping	€1-2
Concierge	Not expected
Taxi Driver	10%

Personal Security

While crime in Lisbon's centre is very low, pickpockets are common. Take care in crowded tourist areas and on popular tram routes, particularly the 28 and 15. Keep your belongings in a safe place and with you at all times.

If you have anything stolen, report the crime within 24 hours to the nearest police station and take ID with you. Get a copy of the crime report to make an insurance claim. There is a police station specifically for tourists at Praça dos Restauradores, beside the tourist office.

Contact your embassy if you have your passport stolen, or in the event of a serious crime or accident.

Health

Seek medicinal supplies and advice for minor ailments from pharmacies (farmácias), identifiable by a green cross. Pharmacists can dispense a range of drugs that would normally be available only on prescription in many other countries. Each pharmacy displays a card in the window showing the address of the nearest all-night pharmacy.

Emergency medical care in Portugal is free for all EU citizens. If you have an EHIC, present this as soon as possible. You may have to pay after treatment and reclaim the money later. For visitors coming from outside the EU, payment of hospital and other medical expenses is the patient's responsibility, so it is important to arrange comprehensive medical insurance before travelling.

Smoking, Alcohol and Drugs

Smoking is banned in most enclosed public spaces and is a fineable offence, although some bars still allow it.

Portugal has a high alcohol consumption rate, however it is frowned upon to be openly drunk. It is common for Lisboetas to drink on the street outside the bar of purchase.

All drugs are decriminalized in Portugal, but possession of small quantities is considered a public health issue and results in a warning or small fine. Drug-dealers brazenly plying their wares in the city centre can be a small nuisance.

ID

By law you must carry identification with you at all times. A photocopy of your passport should suffice. If stopped by the police you may be asked to report to a police station with the original document.

Local Customs

Lisbon is a tolerant and open-minded city, but as the pressure of tourism grows, small efforts to integrate are increasingly appreciated. If possible, use simple Portuguese phrases and greetings appropriate to the time of day. A much-loved aspect of Portugal is the slow pace of life. This is evident as a pedestrian, at public events and when making social engagements, so try to stifle any impatience and readjust your tempo suitably.

Visiting Churches and Cathedrals

Most churches and cathedrals will not permit visitors during Sunday Mass. Generally, entrance to churches is free, however a fee may apply to enter special areas, like cloisters. Portugal retains a strong Catholic identity. When visiting religious buildings ensure that you are dressed modestly, with knees and shoulders covered.

Mobile Phones and Wi-Fi

Free Wi-Fi is not yet widespread in Portugal, but it can be found in some restaurants and bars, specifically those aimed at tourists. Visitors travelling to Portugal with EU tariffs are able to use their devices abroad without being affected by roaming charges. Users will be charged the same rates for data, calls and texts as at home.

Post

The postal service is run by **CTT** (Correios de Portugal), which offers a wide range of services at prices lower than the European average. Stamps are sold in post offices, newsagents and on the CTT website. Post should take around 3–5 days to reach the rest of Europe, 7 days for elsewhere in the world and can be tracked on the **CTT** website, where you can also find details of your nearest post office. There is also a choice of international couriers.

CTT
w ctt.pt

Taxes and Refunds

VAT is usually 23 per cent. Under certain conditions, non-EU citizens can claim a rebate. Either claim the rebate before you buy (show your passport to the shop assistant and complete a form) or claim it retrospectively by presenting a customs officer with your receipts as you leave.

Discount Cards

If you plan to pack a lot of sightseeing into a short trip, purchasing an official **Lisboa Card** can be a cost-efficient choice. For €19, adults receive 24 hours of free public transport, which includes the train lines to Cascais and Sintra; free entry to 26 museums and points of interest; and discounts relating to tours, shopping and nightlife. Cards lasting 48 and 72 hours are also available (€32/€40). The cards can be bought online, at the airport and in the tourist information offices at Praça do Comércio and Praça dos Restauradores.

Lisboa Card
w lisboacard.org

WEBSITES AND APPS

Citymapper
Covers all urban modes of transport, including cycling and walking routes, to help you navigate the city.

Guia de Viagem Visit Portugal
An app showing points of interest nearby or by category.

Lisboa MOVE-ME
A useful app for navigating Lisbon's public transport system.

Lisbon Street Art
An app showing the location of Lisbon's street art.

INDEX

PHRASE BOOK

IN EMERGENCY

Help!	Socorro!	soo-**koh**-roo
Stop!	Páre!	pahr'
Call a doctor!	Chame um médico!	**shahm**'ooñ **meh**-dee-koo
Call an ambulance!	Chame uma ambulância!	**shahm**'oo-muh añ-boo-lañ-see-uh
Call the police!	Chame a polícia!	**shahm**'uh poo-**lee**-see-uh
Call the fire brigade!	Chame os bombeiros!	**shahm**'oosh bom-**bay**-roosh
Where is the nearest telephone?	Há um telefone aqui perto?	ah ooñ te-le-**fon**' uh-**keepehr**-too
Where is the nearest hospital?	Onde é o hospital mais próximo?	ond' eh oo ohsh-pee-**tahl**' mysh pro-see-moo

COMMUNICATION ESSENTIALS

English	Portuguese	Pronunciation
Yes	Sim	seeñ
No	Não	nowñ
Please	Por favor/ Faz favor	poor fuh-**vor** fash fuh-**vor**
Thank you	Obrigado/da	o-bree-**gah**-doo/duh
Excuse me	Desculpe	dish-**koolp**'
Hello	Olá	oh-**lah**
Goodbye	Adeus	a-**deh**-oosh
Good morning	Bom-dia	boñ **dee**-uh
Good afternoon	Boa-tarde	boh-uh tard'
Good night	Boa-noite	boh-uh noyt'
Yesterday	Ontem	oñ-**tayñ**
Today	Hoje	ohj'
Tomorrow	Amanhã	ah-mañ-**yañ**
Here	Aqui	uh-**kee**
There	Ali	uh-**lee**
What?	O quê?	oo keh
Which?	Qual?	kwahl'
When?	Quando?	**kwañ**-doo
Why?	Porquê?	poor-**keh**
Where?	Onde?	oñd'

USEFUL PHRASES

How are you?	Como está?	koh-moo shtah
Very well, thank you.	Bem, obrigado/da.	bayñ o-bree-**gah**-doo/duh
Pleased to meet you.	Encantado/a.	eñ-kañ-**tah**-doo/duh
See you soon.	Até logo.	uh-**teh loh**-goo
That's fine.	Está bem.	shtah bayñ
Where is/are ...?	Onde está/estão ... ?	ond' shtah/ shtowñ
How far is it to ...?	A que distância fica ... ?	uh kee dish-tañ-see-uh **fee**-kuh
Which way to ...?	Como se vai para ... ?	koh-moo seh vy puh-ruh
Do you speak English?	Fala inglês?	**fah**-luh eeñ-glehsh
I don't understand.	Não compreendo.	nowñ kom-pree-eñ-doo
Could you speak more slowly please?	Pode falar mais devagar por favor?	pohd' fuh-**lar** mysh d'-va-gar poor fuh-**vor**
I'm sorry.	Desculpe.	dish-**koolp**'

USEFUL WORDS

big	grande	grañd'
small	pequeno	pe-**keh**-noo
hot	quente	keñt'
cold	frio	free-oo
good	bom	boñ
bad	mau	**mah**-oo
quite a lot/enough	bastante	bash-**tañt**'
well	bem	bayñ
open	aberto	a-**behr**-too
closed	fechado	fe-**shah**-doo
left	esquerda	shkehr-duh
right	direita	dee-**ray**-tuh
straight on	em frente	ayñ freñt'
near	perto	pehr-too
far	longe	loñj'
up	para cima	pur-ruh **see**-muh
down	para baixo	pur-ruh **buy**-shoo
early	cedo	**seh**-doo
late	tarde	tard'
entrance	entrada	eñ-**trah**-duh
exit	saída	sa-**ee**-duh
toilets	casa de banho	kah-zuh d' **bañ**-yoo
more	mais	mysh
less	menos	**meh**-noosh

MAKING A TELEPHONE CALL

I'd like to place an international call.	Queria fazer uma chamada internacional.	kree-uh fuh-**zehr** oo-muh sha-**mah**-duh in-ter-na-**see**-oo-nahl'
a local call.	uma chamada local.	oo-muh sha-**mah**-duh loo-kahl'
Can I leave a message?	Posso deixar uma mensagem?	**poh**-soo day-shar oo-muh meñ-**sah**-jayñ

SHOPPING

How much does this cost?	Quanto custa isto?	kwañ-too koosh-tuh **eesh**-too
I would like ...	Queria ...	kree-uh
I'm just looking.	Estou só a ver obrigado/a.	shtoh sohuh vehr o-bree-**gah**-doo/uh
Do you take credit cards?	Aceita cartões de crédito?	uh-**say**-tuh kar-**toinsh** de **kreh**-dee-too
What time do you open?	A que horas abre?	uh kee oh-rash **ah**-bre
What time do you close?	A que horas fecha?	uh kee oh-rash **fay**-shuh
This one	Este	ehst'
That one	Esse	ehss'
expensive	caro	**kah**-roo
cheap	barato	buh-**rah**-too
size (clothes/shoes)	tamanho	ta-**man**-yoo
white	branco	**brañ**-koo
black	preto	**preh**-too
red	vermelho	ver-**mehl**-yoo
yellow	amarelo	uh-muh-**reh**-loo
green	verde	vehrd'
blue	azul	uh-**zool**'

TYPES OF SHOP

antique shop	loja de antiguidades	**loh**-juh de añ-tee-gwee-**dahd**'sh
bakery	padaria	pah-duh-**ree**-uh
bank	banco	**bañ**-koo
bookshop	livraria	lee-vruh-**ree**-uh
butcher	talho	**tah**-lyoo
cake shop	pastelaria	pash-te-luh-**ree**-uh
chemist	farmácia	far-**mah**-see-uh
fishmonger	peixaria	pay-shuh-**ree**-uh
hairdresser	cabeleireiro	kab'-lay-ray-roo
market	mercado	mehr-**kah**-doo
newsagent	quiosque	kee-**yohsk**'
post office	correios	koo-**ray**-oosh
shoe shop	sapataria	suh-puh-tuh-**ree**-uh
supermarket	supermercado	soo-**pehr**-mer-**kah**-doo
tobacconist	tabacaria	tuh-buh-kuh-**ree**-uh
travel agency	agência de viagens	uh-**jen**-see-uh de vee-**ah**-jayñsh

SIGHTSEEING

English	Portuguese	Pronunciation
cathedral	sé	seh
church	igreja	ee-**gray**-juh
garden	jardim	jar-**deeñ**
library	biblioteca	bee-blee-oo-**teh**-kuh
museum	museu	moo-**zeh**-oo
tourist information office	posto de turismo	**posh**-too d' too-**reesh**-moo
closed for holidays	fechado para férias	fe-**sha**-doo puh-ruh **feh**-ree-ash
bus station	estação de autocarros	shta-**sowñ** d' oh-too-kah-roosh
railway station	estação de comboios	shta-**sowñ** d' koñ-**boy**-oosh

STAYING IN A HOTEL

Do you have a vacant room?	Tem um quarto livre?	tayñ ooñ **kwar**-too leevr'
room with a bath	um quarto com casa de banho	ooñ **kwar**-too koñ **kah**-zuh d' **bañ**-yoo
shower	duche	doosh
single room	quarto individual	**kwar**-too een-dee-vee-doo-**ahl**'
double room	quarto de casal	**kwar**-too d' kuh-**zahl**'
twin room	quarto com duas camas	**kwar**-too koñ **doo**-ash **kah**-mash
porter	porteiro	poor-**tay**-roo
key	chave	shahv'
I have a reservation.	Tenho um quarto reservado.	**tayñ**-yoo ooñ **kwar**-too re-ser-**vah**-doo

EATING OUT

English	Portuguese	Pronunciation
Have you got a table for ...?	Tem uma mesa para ...?	tayñ oo-muh **meh**-zuh puh-ruh

I want to reserve a table.	Quero reservar uma mesa.	keh-roo re-zehr-var oo-muh meh-zuh
The bill please.	A conta por favor/ faz favor.	uh kohn-tuh poor fuh-vor/ fash fuh-vor
I am a vegetarian.	Sou vegetariano/a.	Soh ve-je-tuh-ree-ah-noo/uh
Waiter!	Por favor!/ Faz Favor!	poor fuh-vor fash fuh-vor
the menu	a lista	uh leesh-tuh
fixed-price menu	a ementa turística	uh ee-mehñ-tuh too-reesh-tee-kuh
wine list	a lista de vinhos	uh leesh-tuh de veeñ-yoosh
glass	um copo	ooñ koh-poo
bottle	uma garrafa	oo-muh guh-rah-fuh
half bottle	meia-garrafa	may-uh guh-rah-fuh
knife	uma faca	oo-muh fah-kuh
fork	um garfo	ooñ gar-foo
spoon	uma colher	oo-muh kool-yair
plate	um prato	ooñ prah-too
napkin	um guardanapo	ooñgoo-ar-duh-nah-poo
breakfast	pequeno-almoço	pe-keh-noo-ahl-moh-soo
lunch	almoço	ahl-moh-soo
dinner	jantar	jan-tar
cover	couvert	koo-vehr
starter	entrada	eñ-trah-duh
main course	prato principal	prah-too prin-see-pahl'
dish of the day	prato do dia	prah-too doo dee-uh
set dish	combinado	koñ-bee-nah-doo
half portion	meia-dose	may-uh doh-se
dessert	sobremesa	soh-bre-meh-zuh
rare	mal passado	mahl'puh-sah-doo
medium	médio	meh-dee-oo
well done	bem passado	bayñ puh-sah-doo

MENU DECODER

abacate	uh-buh-kaht'	avocado
açorda	uh-sor-duh	bread-based stew (often seafood)
açúcar	uh-soo-kar	sugar
água mineral	ah-gwuh mee-ne-rahl'	mineral water
(com gás)	koñ gas	sparkling
(sem gás)	sayñ gas	still
alho	al-yoo	garlic
alperce	ahl'-pehrce	apricot
amêijoas	uh-may-joo-ash	clams
ananás	uh-nuh-nahsh	pineapple
arroz	uh-rohsh	rice
assado	uh-sah-doo	baked
atum	uh-tooñ	tuna
aves	ah-vesh	poultry
azeite	uh-zayt'	olive oil
azeitonas	uh-zay-toh-nash	olives
bacalhau	buh-kuh-lyow	dried, salted cod
banana	buh-nah-nuh	banana
batatas	buh-tah-tash	potatoes
batatas fritas	buh-tah-tash free-tash	french fries
batido	buh-tee-doo	milk-shake
bica	bee-kuh	espresso
bife	beef	steak
bolacha	boo-lah-shuh	biscuit
bolo	boh-loo	cake
borrego	boo-reh-goo	lamb
caça	kah-ssuh	game
café	kuh-feh	coffee
camarões	kuh-muh-roysh	large prawns
caracóis	kuh-ruh-koysh	snails
caranguejo	kuh-rañ-gay-joo	crab
carne	karn'	meat
cataplana	kuh-tuh-plah-nuh	sealed wok used to steam dishes
cebola	se-boh-luh	onion
cerveja	sehr-vay-juh	beer
chá	shah	tea
cherne	shern'	stone bass
chocolate	shoh-koh-laht'	chocolate
chocos	shoh-koosh	cuttlefish
chouriço	shoh-ree-soo	red, spicy sausage
churrasco	shoo-rash-coo	on the spit
cogumelos	koo-goo-meh-loosh	mushrooms
cozido	koo-zee-doo	boiled
enguias	eñ-gee-ash	eels
fiambre	fee-añbr'	ham
fígado	fee-guh-doo	liver
frango	frañ-goo	chicken
frito	free-too	fried
fruta	froo-tuh	fruit
gambas	gam-bash	prawns
gelado	je-lah-doo	ice cream
gelo	jeh-loo	ice
goraz	goo-rash	bream
grelhado	grel-yah-doo	grilled
iscas	eesh-kash	marinated liver
lagosta	luh-gohsh-tuh	lobster
laranja	luh-rañ-juh	orange
leite	layt'	milk
limão	lee-mowñ	lemon
limonada	lee-moo-nah-duh	lemonade
linguado	leeñ-gwah-doo	sole
lulas	loo-lash	squid
maçã	muh-sañ	apple
manteiga	mañ-tay-guh	butter
mariscos	muh-reesh-koosh	seafood
meia-de-leite	may-uh-d'layt'	white coffee
ostras	osh-trash	oysters
ovos	oh-voosh	eggs
pão	powñ	bread
pastel	pash-tehl'	cake
pato	pah-too	duck
peixe	paysh'	fish
peixe-espada	paysh'-shpah-duh	scabbard fish
pimenta	pee-meñ-tuh	pepper
polvo	pohl'-voo	octopus
porco	por-coo	pork
queijo	kay-joo	cheese
sal	sahl'	salt
salada	suh-lah-duh	salad
salsichas	sahl-see-shash	sausages
sandes	sañ-desh	sandwich
santola	sañ-toh-luh	spider crab
sopa	soh-puh	soup
sumo	soo-moo	juice
tamboril	tañ-boo-ril'	monkfish
tarte	tart'	pie/cake
tomate	too-maht'	tomato
torrada	too-rah-duh	toast
tosta	tohsh-tuh	toasted sandwich
vinagre	vee-nah-gre	vinegar
vinho branco	veeñ-yoo brañ-koo	white wine
vinho tinto	veeñ-yoo teeñ-too	red wine
vitela	vee-teh-luh	veal

NUMBERS

0	zero	zeh-roo
1	um	ooñ
2	dois	doysh
3	três	tresh
4	quatro	kwa-troo
5	cinco	seeñ-koo
6	seis	saysh
7	sete	set'
8	oito	oy-too
9	nove	nov'
10	dez	desh
11	onze	oñz'
12	doze	doz'
13	treze	trez'
14	catorze	ka-torz'
15	quinze	keeñz'
16	dezasseis	de-zuh-saysh
17	dezassete	de-zuh-set'
18	dezoito	de-zoy-too
19	dezanove	de-zuh-nov'
20	vinte	veent'
21	vinte e um	veen-tee-ooñ
30	trinta	treeñ-tuh
40	quarenta	kwa-reñ-tuh
50	cinquenta	seen-kweñ-tuh
60	sessenta	se-señ-tuh
70	setenta	se-teñ-tuh
80	oitenta	oy-teñ-tuh
90	noventa	noo-veñ-tuh
100	cem	sayñ
101	cento e um	señ-too-ee-ooñ
102	cento e dois	señ-too ee doysh
200	duzentos	doo-zeñ-toosh
300	trezentos	tre-zeñ-toosh
400	quatrocentos	kwa-troo-señ-toosh
500	quinhentos	kee-nyeñ-toosh
700	setecentos	set'-señ-toosh
900	novecentos	nov'-señ-toosh
1,000	mil	meel'

TIME

one minute	um minuto	ooñ mee-noo-too
one hour	uma hora	oo-muh oh-ruh
half an hour	meia-hora	may-uh-oh-ruh
Monday	segunda-feira	se-goon-duh-fay-ruh
Tuesday	terça-feira	ter-sa-fay-ruh
Wednesday	quarta-feira	kwar-ta-fay-ruh
Thursday	quinta-feira	keen-ta-fay-ruh
Friday	sexta-feira	say-shta-fay-ruh
Saturday	sábado	sah-ba-doo
Sunday	domingo	doo-meen-go

ACKNOWLEDGMENTS

The publisher would like to thank the following for their kind permission to reproduce their photographs:

Key: a-above; b-below/bottom; c-centre; f-far; l-left; r-right; t-top

123RF.com: ermess 50cla; manganganath 100b; Sean Pavone 85cla; seregalsv 119tl; Figurniy Sergey 30br; Michael Spring 145bl; sytnik 50cra.

4Corners: Anna Serrano 46br; Luigi Vaccarella 2-3.

Michael Abid: 86-7.

Alamy Stock Photo: Mauricio Abreu 48br, 83br, 89b, 111tr; age fotostock 51bl; / Ken Welsh 137clb; Paulo Amorim 30-1t; Juanma Aparicio 155ca; Archive PL 132cl; John Baran 138br; Antoine Barthelemy 29tr; Bildagentur-online / McPhoto-Boyungs 81tc; Dominic Blewett 45cl; Brazil Photo Press 51tl; Michael Brooks 39b, 134cl, 137bl; David Coleman 122tr; UtCon Collection 140bc; Education & Exploration 1 35br, 81tr; Luis Elvas 70tr; Faraway Photos 135tr; Folio Images 55br; Kevin Foy 34-5t; Greta Gabaglio 40bl; Kevin George 29br; GL Archive 54br; Mauritius images GmbH 168-9t; André Vicente Gonçalves 55tr; Granger Historical Picture Archive 53bc, 53br; Jeff Greenberg 132-3b; Emile Haydon 127t; Hemis 22bl, 41clb, 42br, 44bl, 44-5t, 75tr; Peter Herbert 16c, 58-9; Heritage Image Partnership Ltd 52br; Peter Horree 53tl, 54tl; Hufton+Crow-VIEW 46-7t; imageimage 129tl; INTERFOTO 54bl, 126tc; John Kellerman 53clb; Art Kowalsky 38bl, 137crb; David Litschel 10br; Photolocation ltd 67t, 166b; Pictorial Press Ltd 122bc; M.Sobreira 22cr, 102t, 157br; Cro Magnon 19, 148-9; dov makabaw 32-3b; Martin Thomas Photography 20t, 24t, 42-3t; McPHOTO 37tl; Mikehoward 1 90bl; Tuul and Bruno Morandi 12clb, 32-3t; Ilpo Musto 13t; newborn 24cr; nobleIMAGES 8-9; North Wind Picture Archives 54-5t; Ian Patrick 49cla; Sean Pavone 11cr, 52bc; Roman Pesarenko 146tl; Photolocation 3 33cl; Photononstop 8cl; Luis Miguel Lopes Pina 160-1t; David L. Moore - PRT 49b; Alex Ramsay 147cr; Simon Reddy 33crb; Mieneke Andeweg-van Rijn 155cla; robertharding 4, 48-9t; RosalreneBetancourt 10 45br; RosalreneBetancourt 12 36tl; RosalreneBetancourt 3 38-9t; RosalreneBetancourt 7 121t; Chantel Rowe 27crb; Sagaphoto.com / Stephane Gautier 136-7t; Philip Scalia 39cr; Sueddeutsche Zeitung Photo 108bl; WENN UK 40-1t; Westend61 GmbH 75br; Rob Wilkinson 43cb; Jan Wlodarczyk 8cla, 80-1b; Dudley Wood 103b; Xinhua 27bl.

AWL Images: Mauricio Abreu 12-3b.

© Calouste Gulbenkian Foundation, Lisbon: Carlos Azevedo 26bl, 26-7t, 133tc, 134tr; Founder's Collection / Catarina Gomes Ferreira 133tr.

Depositphotos Inc: ingus.kruklitis.gmail.com 20cr; Figurniy Sergey 24bl, 28tl.

Dorling Kindersley: Peter Wilson 70bc.

Dreamstime.com: Allard1 18bl, 130-1; Altezza 29cl; Leonid Andronov 116clb; Vichaya Kiatying-Angsulee 84bl, 162tc; Myoung Bae 141br; Sergio Torres Baus 8clb; Bennymarty 13cr, 159tc, 159tr, 171tl; Ettore Bordieri 156bc; Coplandj 53tr; Phil Darby 88tl; Debu55y 81cra; Pierre Jean Durieu 155tl; Frank Gärtner 50br; Dan Grytsku 152br; Hagen411 43cla; Miguel Angel Morales Hermo 119cl; Vladimir Korostyshevskiy 123b; Mihai-bogdan Lazar 91cra; Olga Lupol 35cl; Mapics 140t; Meinzahn 117cla; Juan Moyano 101tl; Roland Nagy 98-9t; Sean Pavone 12t, 22t, 24crb, 152t, 154bl; Peek Creative Collective 63br, 124-5; Carlos Sanchez Pereyra 65bl; William Perry 71cl, 144t; Beatrice Preve 55crb; Radub85 36b; Antonio Ribeiro 120b; Arseniy Rogov 13br; Rosshelen 10cla, 107b, 142-3; Saiko3p 11t; 66br; Rui G. Santos 146-7b; Sohadiszno 20bl, 82-3t, 85t; Jose I. Soto 159cra; Taiga 162tl; Tigger76 34b; Stefano Valeri 83cl; Wastesoul 106tl; Zts 41br, 50bl, 64-5t, 88bl, 119br, 126b, 133tl, 160b, 167t.

Getty Images: Mauricio Abreu 56-7, 96-7b; AFP Photo / Francisco Leong 51tr; J.M.F. Almeida 51br; AWL Images / Mauricio Abreu 17bl, 92-3; Benoit Bacou 164-5; Paul Bernhardt 51cr; Corbis / Horacio Villalobos 50cl, 50cr; Sebastien Gaborit 172-3; Gamma-Rapho / Herve Gloaguen 55bl; Pedro Gomes 51cl; Jeff Greenberg 31br; Moment / Gene Krasko 6-7; MyLoupe 62bc; PEC Photo 73tl; Andrea Pucci 104-5; Hans Georg Roth 169bl; Sylvain Sonnet 64bl, 71b, 72br; Alexander Spatari 10-1b, 22crb; Moritz Wolf 62bl.

Grupo José Avillez: Bruno Calado 20crb; Boa Onda 106bc.

iStockphoto.com: diatrezor 62clb; e55evu 18t, 112-3; fjvsoares 11br; Gregobagel 162-3b; hsvrs 139t; LordRunar 17t, 76-7; luniversa 117tr; pasikolkkala 47br; SeanPavonePhoto 68-9, 156cb; soniabonet 109cr; Jacek Sopotnicki 37c; THEPALMER 52t,; urf 117tl; Vertigo3d 31cl; vins_m 111br; Visual_Intermezzo 47cb.

© Museu Nacional de Arte Antiga, Lisboa Instituto dos Museus e da Conservação - MC: Paulo Alexandrino 96clb, 97tl, 97tr, 97cla, 98bl, 99tr, 99clb.

Museu da Marioneta: Andre é Boto 102bc.

Museu do Fado: José Frade 66tl.

1/16

Shutterstock: Zambad06 28-9b.

SuperStock: age fotostock / Eduardo Grund 156bl; Hemis / Pierre Jaques 134-5b; Maurìcio Abreu 37br.

Front flap:
Alamy Stock Photo: Antoine Barthelemy bl, Hufton+Crow-VIEW t, Photononstop cla, Luis Miguel Lopes Pina cb; **Dreamstime.com:** Sergio Torres Baus br; **Getty Images:** Alexander Spatari cra.

Cover images:
Front and spine: **Alamy Stock Photo:** Sean Pavone.
Back: **Alamy Stock Photo:** Art Kowalsky c, Sean Pavone b, Jan Wlodarczyk cla; **Getty Images:** Alexander Spatari tr.

For further information see www.dkimages.com

MIX
Paper from responsible sources
FSC www.fsc.org FSC™ C018179

The information in this DK Eyewitness Travel Guide is checked regularly.
Every effort has been made to ensure that this book is as up-to-date as possible at the time of going to press. Some details, however, such as telephone numbers, opening hours, prices, gallery hanging arrangements and travel information, are liable to change. The publishers cannot accept responsibility for any consequences arising from the use of this book, nor for any material on third party websites, and cannot guarantee that any website address in this book will be a suitable source of travel information. We value the views and suggestions of our readers very highly. Please write to: Publisher, DK Eyewitness Travel Guides, Dorling Kindersley, 80 Strand, London, WC2R 0RL, UK, or email: travelguides@dk.com

DK | Penguin Random House

Main Contributers Matthew Hancock and Mandy Tomlin, Andy Gregory, Susie Boulton, Sarah McAlister
Senior Editor Ankita Awasthi Tröger
Senior Designer Owen Bennett
Project Editors Rachel Thompson, Lucy Sienkowska
Project Art Editors Dan Bailey, Tania Gomes, Vinita Venugopal, Bharti Karakoti, Hansa Babra, Ankita Sharma
Design Assistant William Robinson

Lisbon
5941141

London Borough of Southwark
SK 2691236 8
A & H | 22-Jan-2019
914.6942 TRAV | £12.99
CW

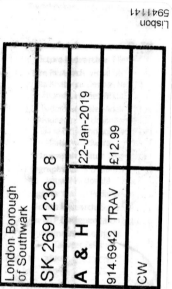

First edition 1997

Published in Great Britain by Dorling Kindersley Limited, 80 Strand, London, WC2R 0RL

Published in the United States by DK Publishing, 345 Hudson Street, New York, New York 10014

Copyright © 1997, 2019 Dorling Kindersley Limited
A Penguin Random House Company
19 20 21 22 10 9 8 7 6 5 4 3 2 1

All rights reserved.

No part of this publication may be reproduced, stored in or introduced into a retrieval system, or transmitted, in any form, or by any means (electronic, mechanical, photocopying, recording, or otherwise), without the prior written permission of the copyright owner.

A CIP catalogue record for this book is available from the British Library.

A catalog record for this book is available from the Library of Congress.

ISSN: 1542 1554
ISBN: 978 0 2413 5831 3

Printed and bound in China.

www.dk.com